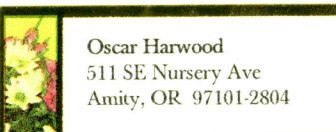

Oscar Harwood
511 SE Nursery Ave
Amity, OR 97101-2804

A LIVING HOPE

GEORGE E. RICE

Pacific Press Publishing Association
Boise, Idaho
Oshawa, Ontario, Canada

Edited by Bonnie Widicker
Designed by Tim Larson
Cover illustrations by James Converse and John Steel
Typeset in 10/12 Century Schoolbook

Copyright © 1992 by
Pacific Press Publishing Association
Printed in United States of America
All Rights Reserved

The author assumes full responsibility for the accuracy of the facts and quotations cited in this book.

Library of Congress Cataloging-in-Publication-Data:
Rice, George E., 1933-
   A living hope: 1 Peter / by George E. Rice.
      p.   cm.
   Includes bibliographical references.
   ISBN 0-8163-1065-3
   1. Bible. N.T. Peter, 1st—Criticism, interpretation, etc.
   2. Peter, the Apostle, Saint. I. Title.
   BS2795.2.R53 1991
   227'.9206—dc20   91-31721
                                                              CIP

Dedication

To my parents
George H. and Dorothy L. Rice

Contents

Chapter	1	Peter: First Among Equals	7
Chapter	2	Elect Strangers and Pilgrims	17
Chapter	3	Our Living Hope	25
Chapter	4	The Triumph of Faith	35
Chapter	5	Call to Holy Living	45
Chapter	6	God's Showcase	55
Chapter	7	Civic Responsibilities	63
Chapter	8	Walking in His Footsteps	73
Chapter	9	To Love, Honor, and Cherish	81
Chapter	10	Defend the Faith	89
Chapter	11	Victory and Service	99
Chapter	12	Suffering and the Christian	109
Chapter	13	Final Exhortations	119

Chapter 1

Peter: First Among Equals

Matthew 16:13-20; Acts 1:15-23; Mark 14:66-72; John 21:15-19; Acts 9:32-43

Some people find making new acquaintances an exciting experience. At every opportunity they engage strangers in conversation, wanting to know their names, where they are from, what they do for a living, and how many children or grandchildren they have. Because these people are so friendly and open, it is hard to resist them.

Learning new things about people you already know is equally exciting. I found this out at a social event where I thought I knew everyone, only to discover that one woman had won a state championship for stilt walking when she was a teenager and that a man who was present had climbed to the highest point of the Golden Gate bridge while it was under construction.

This principle can be transferred to Bible characters. Some we just don't know, and discovering information about them makes them real for us. Others are very familiar to us, and when we discover something new about them, we feel as though a friendship has been deepened. From the twelve apostles, Peter is perhaps the best known. But we can learn new things about him that will help us know him better.

First Among Apostles

Besides being named first in all the apostolic lists (Matthew 10:1-4; Mark 3:16-19; Luke 6:13-16; Acts 1:13), Peter has the distinction of being first in a number of other categories.

First fruit of another man's labor. According to the Gospel account (John 1:35-42), Peter is the first convert won to Christ as the result of another man's labor. Andrew, Peter's brother, together with the beloved disciple John, had already spent the day in a private interview with Jesus. Under deep conviction, Andrew left the place where Jesus was staying and immediately sought out his brother. "We have found the Messias," Andrew blurted out (verse 41). Then he introduced Peter to Jesus. It would seem that Peter will not be the only star in Andrew's crown, however. Verse 41 tells us that Andrew "first findeth his own brother Simon." Is it possible that others were brought to Jesus as a result of Andrew's efforts?

First called to the gospel ministry. Although Peter was introduced to Jesus and became one of His disciples shortly after Jesus' baptism, it was not until a year and a half later that Peter was called to full-time ministry. According to the Synoptic Gospels (Matthew 4:18-22; Mark 1:16-20; Luke 5:1-11), the call came by the Sea of Galilee, and Peter was the first to accept the invitation.

There is no contradiction between John's account of Peter's first meeting with Jesus and the call to full-time ministry in Matthew, Mark, and Luke. Eighteen months separated these two events, and it was at the time when John the Baptist was arrested that Peter was called to ministry. Concerning the call by the sea, Ellen White says:

> Until this time none of the disciples had fully united as colaborers with Jesus. They had witnessed many of His miracles, and had listened to His teaching; but they had not entirely forsaken their former employment. . . . But now Jesus called them to forsake their former life,

and unite their interests with His.[1]

First among the triumvirate. The disciples divided themselves naturally into three groups. From the Twelve, Peter, Andrew, James, John, Philip, Nathanael, and Matthew had been closer to Jesus than the rest. From this group, Peter, James, and John formed the triumvirate. They were almost constantly with Jesus.[2] Therefore, they were granted opportunities the other nine did not share. For example, they were taken into the chamber of death and allowed to witness the resurrection of Jairus's daughter (Mark 5:35-43). They were permitted to see the moment of glory and the moment of agony—the Transfiguration (Matthew 17:1-13) and Gethsemane (Matthew 26:36-46).

That Peter was the leader of the triumvirate can be seen in his responses and reactions. On the way to Jairus's house, Peter responded on behalf of all by saying, "Master, the multitude throng thee and press thee, and sayest thou, Who touched me?" (Luke 8:45). On the Mount of Transfiguration, the leader spoke, "Lord, it is good for us to be here" (Matthew 17:4), and in the garden, Peter asserted his leadership with the sword, perhaps intending to inspire courage in the hearts of the other disciples to defend their Lord (John 18:10).

First apostle to see the resurrected Lord. When the two disciples who had made the trek to Emmaus returned to Jerusalem, expecting to announce the glad tidings that they had seen the Lord, they were greeted by the joyous proclamation of the apostles, "The Lord is risen indeed, and hath appeared to Simon" (Luke 24:34). Paul confirmed this experience many years later when he wrote to the Corinthians, "He was seen of Cephas, then of the twelve" (1 Corinthians 15:5).

First to preach salvation for the Gentiles. Jesus repeatedly taught the apostles that the kingdom is open to any Gentile who accepts the provision provided for entrance. We generally think of Paul as the apostle who carried these tidings to the non-Jewish world. However, it is Peter who first proclaimed this grand truth.

As the people responded to Peter's sermon on the Day of

10 A LIVING HOPE

Pentecost, he told his Jewish audience, "The promise is unto you, and to your children, and to all that are afar off" (Acts 2:39). "Afar off" is a rabbinic term used for those who are outside of the covenant—the Gentiles. The Jews, being within the secure boundaries of the covenant, are referred to as "near" (or "nigh," KJV).

Paul uses these rabbinic phrases as he writes to the Gentile Christians in Ephesus: "At that time ye were without Christ, being aliens from the commonwealth of Israel, and strangers from the covenants of promise, having no hope, and without God in the world: but now in Christ Jesus ye who sometimes were far off are made nigh by the blood of Christ." He "came and preached peace to you which were afar off, and to them that were nigh" (Ephesians 2:12, 13, 17).

First to win Gentile converts. Again, Peter is the first apostle to win non-Jewish converts to Christ. He reminded the Christian leaders at the Jerusalem council (A.D. 49) of his work with Cornelius and his household, and that he was the first among the apostles to be chosen by God for this work. "Men and brethren, ye know how that a good while ago God made choice among us, that the Gentiles by my mouth should hear the word of the gospel, and believe" (Acts 15:7).

Peter's major work, however, was to be among his own people. While living in Jerusalem, he worked untiringly for the Jews who came to the Holy City to worship at the time of the annual festivals.[3]

First apostle to preach salvation by faith. The first sermons by an apostle to be recorded in the book of Acts were given by Peter, and they are an interesting insight into the early teaching of the church. Although we generally think of Paul as the great preacher of righteousness by faith, the New Testament sets forth Peter as the first apostle to make this proclamation.

The first three sermons in Acts were addressed to (1) the worshipers on the Day of Pentecost (Acts 2:14-36), (2) the worshipers gathered around the crippled man who had been healed (Acts 3:12-26), and (3) the Sanhedrin upon the arrest of Peter and John after the miraculous healing (Acts 4:8-12).

These sermons on salvation by faith contained three

common elements: (1) the fulfillment of the Abrahamic and Davidic covenants, (2) the proclamation of salvation by faith in Jesus alone, and (3) the proclamation of salvation for the Gentiles.

Review of firsts. Rethink the various ways the Bible writers bring out the prominence of Peter's role among the apostles:

1. He is always named first in the four apostolic lists found in the New Testament. Matthew even attaches the word *first* to Peter's name in his list.

2. He was the first to be brought to Jesus by the efforts of another person.

3. When Jesus called the Twelve to full-time gospel ministry at a later time, Peter was the first to be chosen.

4. He is always named first among the three disciples who were the closest to Jesus.

5. He was the first apostle to see the risen Lord.

6. He was the first apostle sent by God to labor among the Gentiles.

7. He was the first apostle in the New Testament record to proclaim salvation by faith in Jesus alone, as well as salvation for the Gentiles by making them the recipients of the blessings found in the covenant made with Abraham.

The Sifting of Peter

Peter's position as leader among the apostles did not remove him from temptation. Indeed, because of his leadership position, Satan wanted to control Peter so he could sift him as wheat (Luke 22:31); but Jesus had given Peter the assurance that he need not fail: "I have prayed for thee, that thy faith fail not" (Luke 22:32). When the hour of testing had come, Jesus had meekly submitted to the arresting party. He had rebuked Peter when he tried to protect his Master. Hurt and terrified, Peter followed the arresting party at a distance.

At the home of the high priest, Jesus was physically and verbally abused, but He did nothing to defend Himself. The murderous intent of the religious leaders was clear. Jesus was going to die! The realization of what was about to happen flooded over Peter. All the dreams of the restored kingdom, the future glory of Israel, to say nothing of his own personal ambitions—all were lost.

A woman's voice jolted Peter's attention back to the events of the moment: "This man was also with him" (Luke 22:56). We must clarify Peter's response as he was identified the third time before we see the magnitude of what happened. It is generally thought that Peter blasphemed God, i.e., "He began to curse and to swear" (Mark 14:71). However, this is unlikely. Peter knew that such profanity was punishable by stoning. If he lacked the courage to reveal his true identity at Jesus' trial, it is highly unlikely that he would deliberately profane the name of God in the courtyard of the high priest, knowing that such profanity would result in his death by stoning.

If Peter did not blaspheme the name of God, what did he do? An examination of the words *to curse* and *to swear* proves helpful. The Greek word translated *swear* means "to take an oath that what is said is true." This word is followed by the statement alleged to be true. This is the case in Mark 14:71, "He began . . . to swear, saying, I know not this man of whom ye speak." The Greek word translated "curse" means "to pronounce something or someone as worthy of destruction or death."

There is no problem with the word *to swear*. Peter simply took an oath that he was telling the truth when he said he did not know Jesus. The question to be resolved, however, is, Who did Peter pronounce worthy of death? The editors of the RSV present this verse as follows, "But he began to invoke a curse on himself." There is, however, nothing in the grammar of Mark 14:66-72 to warrant the conclusion that Peter called down the curse of death upon himself. The object of the sentence of death is not identified by either Mark or Matthew. Some suggest that the object of Peter's curse of death is Jesus, and the Gospel writers left the object of the curse unspecified, perhaps too ashamed to record it.

By pronouncing the curse of death upon Jesus, Peter endeavored to convince the crowd, "I do not know the man." It was as though Peter joined the crowd and cried, "Crucify Him, crucify Him." While the curse of death was still on Peter's lips,

Jesus turned and look at him—their eyes met.

As Peter stood at the brink—ashamed, horrified at his behavior, abhorring himself—Satan wished to crush him, to engulf him in the darkness of utter despair, to snatch him out of the hands of the Saviour. Ellen White asks a provocative question concerning Peter: "In that hour of anguish and self-abhorrence, what could have held him back from the path trodden by Judas?"[4]

Two things restrained Peter from self-destruction: (1) There was no condemnation on the countenance of Jesus, only pity and compassion. (2) When Jesus had told Peter that Satan was going to sift him, Jesus instilled hope in Peter's heart by assuring him that the Son of God had prayed that his faith would not fail.

Peter's Restoration

By denying his Lord and pronouncing the curse of death upon Him, Peter disqualified himself as a member of that close group known as apostles. However, his repentance was genuine, and a change took place.

The restoration. Peter had publicly disqualified himself to be an apostle. Now he was to be restored to that select group by a public confession. Three times Jesus asked Peter if he loved Him (John 21:15-19), and three times Peter assured Jesus that he did. With each response Jesus gave Peter a commission to care for His sheep. But more is taking place than meets the eye. Unfortunately, the dynamics of this conversation are lost in translation. Let's try to reconstruct the nuances.

The Greek language has four words that are translated *love* in English: (1) sensual love (*erō*); (2) mutual love of parents, children, and friends for each other (*stergō*); (3) love of the Greek gods for humans, regard with affection, love as one's wife (*phileō*); and (4) a little-used word that means nothing more than to be satisfied with something (*agapaō*).

All four words appear in classical Greek, but the New Testament uses only *phileō* and *agapaō*. Strange as it may seem, it is the last word (*agapaō*) that Jesus used for the love God has for fallen human beings (*agapē*). Taking a word seldom used because it failed to express human love, Jesus infused it with new meaning that far surpassed anything that could be conveyed by the other three words—God's love for His earthly children.

When Jesus asked Peter if he loved Him (John 21:15-17), the first two times He used the word that now represents the love that God has for His children (*agapaō*), but Peter replied with *phileō*. Why did Peter do this? Was it because he was accustomed to use the word that commonly designated affection, or was Peter communicating something to Jesus we do not understand in our modern culture? The answer may be found within Roman society.

Society of friends. In Roman society there was a class known as "friends," within which a person of lesser social standing entered into an "intimate" relationship with a person of wealth and power for the benefit of both parties.

For example, a freed slave who did not wish to leave the household of his master might enter into this relationship with his former master and guarantee loyalty to him and his household. The former master, in turn, guaranteed to provide for the material and social needs of the "friend." The affairs of the former master became the affairs of the "friend," and they withheld no secrets from each other. Derek Tidball says, "It was in this way that Augustus built up a system of friends bound by loyalty to him rather than to other seats of power in the Roman Empire."[5] This aspect of Roman society is seen in the New Testament.

Pilate had entered into a relationship with Caesar as his friend (John 19:12); therefore, he had committed himself to protect Caesar's interests and to be loyal to him. He could not afford to have the report reach Rome that he had released a prisoner who had accepted the position and homage of the people as King of the Jews.

Jesus spoke of His relationship with the apostles against the backdrop of the Roman society of friends: "Ye are my friends, if ye do whatsoever I command you. Henceforth I call you not servants; for the servant knoweth not what his lord doeth: but I have called you friends; for all things that I have heard of my Father I have made known unto you" (John 15:14, 15).

It was from this special relationship with Jesus that Peter had disqualified himself. When Jesus asked Peter if he loved Him (*agapaō*), Peter replied with the verb (*phileō*) that forms the base for the word *friend* (*philos*). Thus Peter not only assured Jesus he loved Him, but communicated to Jesus that he loved Him as a true "friend"—as one who would be obediently loyal (see John 15:14).

But the question is, Would the Master accept Peter back as a "friend"? The third time Jesus asked the question, He changed the verb: "Simon, son of Jonas, lovest [*phileō*] thou me?" (John 21:17). This variation assured Peter that he was accepted back into the society of Jesus' "friends."

Summary

"Now the names of the twelve apostles are these; The first, Simon, who is called Peter" (Matthew 10:2). Truly Peter was first among equals. He was aggressive, ambitious, boastful, and cowardly before his conversion, but courageous, distrustful of self, modest, and subdued after his conversion. This is the man who wrote 1 Peter.

---

1. *The Desire of Ages*, pp. 246-249.
2. Ibid., p. 292.
3. *The Acts of the Apostles*, p. 514.
4. *Education*, p. 89.
5. Derek Tidball, *The Social Context of the New Testament* (Grand Rapids: Zondervan Publishing House, 1984), pp. 80, 81.

Chapter 2
Elect Strangers and Pilgrims

1 Peter 1:1, 2; 4:3, 4; 5:12-14

What a joyous fellowship every congregation would experience if only the saints could view one another as Peter sees them—elect of God, sanctified by the power of the Spirit, obedient to the Word of God, and cleansed in the blood of Jesus. This is Peter's perception of his fellow believers (1 Peter 1:1, 2). Can you think of any other group of people you would rather live among?

Whether you believe it or not, the person sitting in the pew beside you is one of God's elect. He or she will be with you in the kingdom, provided you both remain faithful to Jesus, of course. If living with the saints in your congregation is a happy, exciting experience, try to imagine the joy when the church family is expanded to include the redeemed of all ages.

The grand reunion of all the redeemed from planet Earth is pictured by John the revelator in terms of a wedding—an apt image, for weddings are frequently occasions for family reunions. The groom is the Lamb of God (Revelation 21:9); the bride is the holy city, New Jerusalem (21:10); the guests are those who have heard and responded to the call of the gospel

(22:14); and the invitation to the wedding reads as follows: "The Spirit and the bride say, Come" (22:17).

Peter addresses his first letter to those who have either heard or read the invitation and have responded—the elect from all periods of the Christian era.

Elect of God

The idea of being elected or chosen raises serious questions in the minds of some Christians, especially those whose doctrinal beliefs do not have roots in Calvinism. They tend to equate election with predestination—the belief that some are destined to be saved regardless of how they live, and others are destined to be lost even though they live good, moral lives. What does the Bible mean when it speaks in terms of the elect of God?

The concept of election, or being chosen, runs throughout the Bible, but the reader must be careful not to interject preconceived notions into this concept. For example, Israel was elected by God to play a special role among the nations, but this election for service did not guarantee eternal salvation. Neither did they earn the honor of election; it was bestowed upon them:

> The Lord thy God hath chosen thee to be a special people unto himself, above all people that are upon the face of the earth. The Lord did not set his love upon you, nor choose you, because ye were more in number than any people; for ye were the fewest of all people: but because the Lord loved you, and because he would keep the oath which he had sworn unto your fathers (Deuteronomy 7:6-8).

Israel was chosen for their mission because of the covenant that God had made with their forefathers and the relationship that existed within this covenant, not because of their merits or greatness. Israel's privilege of being elected for service within God's plan for the world did not guarantee their eternal salvation:

ELECT STRANGERS AND PILGRIMS 19

> Know therefore that the Lord thy God, he is God, the faithful God, which keepeth covenant and mercy with them that love him and keep his commandments to a thousand generations; and repayeth them that hate him to their face, to destroy them: he will not be slack to him that hateth him, he will repay him to his face. Thou shalt therefore keep the commandments, and the statutes, and the judgments, which I command thee this day, to do them (verses 9-11).

Israel's election did not place them beyond judgment when they disobeyed. Their election only made sin all the more offensive in the eyes of God.

We also read of individuals in the Bible who were elected or chosen by the Lord. To Jeremiah God said, "Before I formed thee in the belly I knew thee; and before thou camest forth out of the womb I sanctified thee, and I ordained thee a prophet unto the nations" (Jeremiah 1:5). In the New Testament we read of John the Baptist, who was elected before his birth, like Jeremiah, to be a prophet of God (Luke 1:5-20). But election to service is no guarantee of salvation.

How vividly the experience of Israel's first king illustrates this principle. Although once elected by God, in utter hopelessness Saul exclaimed just hours before his death, "God is departed from me, and answereth me no more" (1 Samuel 28:15).

While election to service does not guarantee salvation, there is, on the other hand, no salvation without election:

> Wherefore the rather, brethren, give diligence to make your calling and election sure: for if ye do these things, ye shall never fall: for so an entrance shall be ministered unto you abundantly into the everlasting kingdom of our Lord and Saviour Jesus Christ (2 Peter 1:10, 11).

Ellen White says, "There is no such thing as a human being sanctified and fitted for the heavenly kingdom not having an election to that kingdom."[1] She further points out that election is based upon the conditions of faith and obedience:

> The Father sets His love upon His elect people who live in the midst of men. These are the people whom Christ has redeemed by the price of His own blood; and because they respond to the drawing of Christ, through the sovereign mercy of God, they are elected to be saved as His obedient children. . . . Everyone who will humble himself as a little child, who will receive and obey the Word of God with a child's simplicity, will be among the elect of God.[2]

The condition of obedience is further emphasized in the following words:

> You are elected to wear the yoke of Christ—to bear His burden, to lift His cross. You are to be diligent "to make your calling and election sure." Search the Scriptures, and you will see that not a son or a daughter of Adam is elected to be saved in disobedience to God's law. The world makes void the law of God; but Christians are chosen to sanctification through obedience to the truth. They are elected to bear the cross, if they would wear the crown.[3]

Nothing can be more emphatic than the following: "There is no such thing in the Word of God as unconditional election—once in grace, always in grace."[4]

Predestined

If there is no such thing as unconditional election, where do people get the idea of predestination? They get it from the Bible, for the teaching of predestination is, indeed, present in Scripture. But we must read these passages carefully to see what is predestined. For example, Romans 8:29 says, "For whom he did foreknow, he also did predestinate to be conformed to the image of his Son, that he might be the firstborn among many brethren."

This verse contains two points of interest: (1) God, in His omniscience, knows beforehand who will be His faithful children, and (2) He has predestined that they bear the image of

His Son. However, having prior knowledge of our eternal destiny does not fix that destiny. Otherwise we would not have freedom of choice, which is the one commodity that God preserves for all humans within the context of the great controversy. If this freedom were to be taken from us, Satan would cry, "Foul!" and his charges that God is unjust and tyrannical would stand as truth.

God has also "predestinated us unto the adoption of children by Jesus Christ to himself, according to the good pleasure of his will" (Ephesians 1:5). And he has also "predestinated according to the purpose of him who worketh all things after the counsel of his own will: That we should be to the praise of his glory, who first trusted in Christ" (verses 11, 12).

So we see in Scripture that God has predestined that those who believe in Jesus will: (1) bear the image of His Son, (2) be adopted as His children, and (3) live to the praise of His glory.

Ellen White says, "The predestination of which God speaks includes all who will accept Christ as a personal Saviour, who will return to their loyalty, to perfect obedience to all God's commandments."[5] Therefore, election and predestination by God are conditional upon the exercise of our free choice. This is borne out in the following statement: "Those who perish will perish because they refuse to be adopted [something that God has predestined, Ephesians 1:5] as children of God through Christ Jesus."[6]

Strangers and Pilgrims

Peter addresses his first epistle to the strangers who are scattered throughout the area now known as Turkey. Chances are, these people were not strangers or exiles as we think of these terms today. They had not been uprooted from their homeland and transported into a foreign country, but most likely had always lived in the very cities and towns in which they were living when Peter addressed his epistle to them.

In what sense, then, could they possibly be strangers? Having accepted God's saving grace and having been adopted into His family, they joined the band of elect pilgrims who do not count this world as their home but press onward in their spiritual journey toward the eternal goal. They were now strangers to the ways of the world—saints living in the environment of sin but not a part of that environment, pilgrims in a dreary land.

As Peter himself says, "Let the time that is past suffice for doing what the Gentiles like to do, living in licentiousness, passions, drunkenness, revels, carousing, and lawless idolatry. They are surprised that you do not now join them in the same wild profligacy, and they abuse you" (1 Peter 4:3, 4, RSV).

Peter, the disciple, simply passed on a spiritual principle taught by the Master Teacher: "If the world hate you, ye know that it hated me before it hated you. If ye were of the world, the world would love his own: but because ye are not of the world, but I have chosen you out of the world, therefore the world hateth you" (John 15:18, 19).

The pilgrim theme runs throughout the Old and New Testaments. Abraham, the spiritual father of those who believe, is the great pilgrim image of the Bible:

> By faith Abraham, when he was called to go out into a place which he should after receive for an inheritance, obeyed; and he went out, not knowing whither he went. By faith he sojourned in the land of promise, as in a strange country, dwelling in tabernacles with Isaac and Jacob, the heirs with him of the same promise: for he looked for a city which hath foundations, whose builder and maker is God" (Hebrews 11:8-10).

And so, those who believe, being children of Abraham (Galatians 3:7, 29), are pilgrims with him in a hostile world.

Because the elect of God are pilgrims in the environment of sin, Bible writers call them to a way of life that testifies that they are indeed strangers in this world. God's people are to be different. They are not to live like the world nor look like the world. Their lifestyle is to testify that they belong to Jesus. The apostle Paul describes it this way:

> This I say therefore, and testify in the Lord, that ye

henceforth walk not as other Gentiles walk, in the vanity of their mind, having the understanding darkened, being alienated from the life of God through the ignorance that is in them, because of the blindness of their heart: who being past feeling have given themselves over unto lasciviousness, to work all uncleanness with greediness. But ye have not so learned Christ; if so be that ye have heard him, and have been taught by him as the truth is in Jesus: that ye put off concerning the former conversation the old man, which is corrupt according to the deceitful lusts; and be renewed in the spirit of your mind; and that ye put on the new man, which after God is created in righteousness and true holiness.

Let all bitterness, and wrath, and anger, and clamour, and evil speaking, be put away from you, with all malice: and be ye kind one to another, tenderhearted, forgiving one another, even as God for Christ's sake hath forgiven you (Ephesians 4:17-24, 31, 32).

The entire orientation of the elect pilgrims differs from the orientation of those who choose the world. Paul summarizes this orientation when he says:

Finally, brethren, whatsoever things are true, whatsoever things are honest, whatsoever things are just, whatsoever things are pure, whatsoever things are lovely, whatsoever things are of good report; if there be any virtue, and if there be any praise, think on these things (Philippians 4:8).

As the pilgrims of God commit themselves to this orientation, the Holy Spirit comes to their aid:

Having brought conviction of sin, and presented before the mind the standard of righteousness, the Holy Spirit withdraws the affections from the things of this earth and fills the soul with a desire for holiness. . . . The Spirit will take the things of God and stamp them on the soul.[7]

24 A LIVING HOPE

The pilgrims focus on the coming of our Lord. If anything turns us away from the sinful, frivolous lifestyle of this present age, it should be the hope of Jesus' return. When this hope burns bright within the hearts of His people, they will be distinct from those who do not have this hope.

> The second coming of the Son of man is to be the wonderful theme kept before the people. Here is a subject that should not be left out of our discourses. Eternal realities must be kept before the mind's eyes, and the attractions of the world will appear as they are, altogether profitless as vanity. What are we to do with the world's vanities, its praises, its riches, its honors, or its enjoyments?
>
> We are pilgrims and strangers who are waiting, hoping, and praying for that blessed hope, the glorious appearing of our Lord and Saviour Jesus Christ. If we believe this and bring it into our practical life, what vigorous action would this faith and hope inspire; what fervent love one for another; what careful holy living for the glory of God; and in our respect for the recompense of the reward, what distinct lines of demarcation would be evidenced between us and the world.[8]

Lift up your eyes, weary pilgrim, hold your head high, for we are almost home.

---

1. *Seventh-day Adventist Bible Commentary,* vol. 7, p. 944.
2. Ibid., vol. 6, p. 1114.
3. *Fundamentals of Christian Education*, p. 126.
4. *Seventh-day Adventist Bible Commentary*, vol. 6, p. 1114.
5. *Manuscript Releases*, vol. 6, p. 388.
6. *Seventh-day Adventist Bible Commentary*, vol. 6, p. 1114.
7. *The Acts of the Apostles*, pp. 52, 53.
8. *Evangelism*, p. 220.

Chapter 3
Our Living Hope

1 Peter 1:3-5

At some time or other, we all have heard stories that have tugged at our hearts. I remember hearing Lincoln Steffens's "A Miserable, Merry Christmas" when I was a mere boy. I think the story stuck in my mind because I identified so closely with the main character—a boy about my age with similar interests.

To summarize a long story of dashed hopes and a happy ending: As Christmas approached, young Lincoln Steffens had set his heart on a pony. When he made his Christmas wish known to his parents, they did nothing to encourage their son's hopes. All the boy could think of and talk about was the pony he wanted. There was plenty of room for it in the stable, and the boy rehearsed his wishes to his parents and to God. He went so far as to declare that if he couldn't have a pony, he wanted nothing at all.

On Christmas morning, Lincoln and his sisters dashed downstairs to open presents before the parents were up. The girls' stuffed stockings were surrounded by presents. Lincoln's stocking dangled limply, all by itself. After crying for a while—Lincoln in disappointment, the girls in sympathy—he dressed, went to the empty stable, and wept some more. He ignored his mother's urging to join the family for Christmas breakfast.

Instead, he sat on the front steps, feeling wronged and hurt. He would see his father peeking through the curtains every little while, but he paid no attention to him. After some time, he saw a man riding down the street on a small horse with a brand-new boy's saddle. He knew it was a boy's saddle because the man's legs were too long, and his feet were not in the stirrups. Such a horse and saddle were the exact object of the boy's dreams. As the man rode on past the house, Lincoln broke into tears again, feeling the hurt of dashed hopes more keenly than before. His weeping was interrupted, however, by a man's voice asking if he knew where a kid named Lennie Steffens lived. Looking up, he saw the horse and the long-legged man. He had had difficulty delivering the horse because the house number wasn't visible from the road. Lincoln's loving parents had planned carefully to fulfill his Christmas dream. But its delayed arrival brought the boy disappointment and heartbreak before the joy his parents had intended.

Dashed Messianic Hopes

How similar was the experience of the disciples to that of the boy on Christmas morning. The disciples believed that Jesus was Israel's Messiah. They had heard Jesus claim divine sonship. They witnessed miracle after miracle that supported His claim.

On Sunday before the Passover, Jesus had ridden into Jerusalem following the custom of the Davidic kings in the Old Testament. For the first time He permitted the people to proclaim Him as King. In fact, when the religious leaders tried to silence the crowd during the triumphal entry and appealed to Jesus to restore order, He replied, "I tell you that, if these should hold their peace, the stones would immediately cry out" (Luke 19:40).

The time had come for Jesus to assume His position as the King of Israel.

> No sooner was He seated upon the colt than a loud

shout of triumph rent the air. The multitude hailed Him as Messiah, their King. Jesus now accepted the homage which He had never before permitted, and the disciples received this as proof that their glad hopes were to be realized by seeing Him established on the throne.[1]

The following morning the disciples received further evidence that Jesus would now press His claim to David's throne. Having accepted the position as Israel's king, He now acted in that role—He cleansed the temple and took control of its functions.

> In fulfillment of prophecy the people had proclaimed Jesus king of Israel. He had received their homage, and accepted the office of king. In this character He must act. He knew that His efforts to reform a corrupt priesthood would be in vain; nevertheless His work must be done; to an unbelieving people the evidence of His divine mission must be given.[2]

> The Pharisees were utterly perplexed and disconcerted. One whom they could not intimidate was in command. Jesus had taken His position as guardian of the temple. Never before had He assumed such kingly authority.[3]

By Monday night the disciples were riding the crest of a Messianic high. Jesus had thrown down the gauntlet. He had finally accepted the position of king and had taken the temple out of the hands of the corrupt priests. His enemies were powerless before Him. Now the disciples were ready to take on the Romans.

Ah, victory! How fleeting it is! Four nights later, these same men wallowed in dashed hopes and deep depression. The depth of their despair is echoed in the words of the Emmaus disciples: "We trusted that it had been he which should have redeemed Israel" (Luke 24:21).

The disciples could have avoided riding this emotional roller coaster. If only they had listened to Jesus, they could have endured the experience of the crucifixion with their hopes fixed upon the resurrection. Mark tells us that approximately one year before the crucifixion, Jesus began talking about His approaching death: "He began to teach them, that the Son of man must suffer many things, and be rejected of the elders, and of the chief priests, and scribes, and be killed, and after three days rise again" (Mark 8:31). On two later occasions Jesus told the disciples He was to die (Mark 9:31; 10:33, 34). But preconceived opinions and personal ambition would not permit the disciples to hear.

It was their pride of heart, their thirst for worldly glory, that had led them to cling so tenaciously to the false teaching of their time, and to pass unheeded the Saviour's words showing the true nature of His kingdom, and pointing forward to His agony and death.[4]

When Christ was crucified, they did not believe that He would rise. He had stated plainly that He was to rise on the third day, but they were perplexed to know what He meant. This lack of comprehension left them at the time of His death in utter hopelessness. They were bitterly disappointed. Their faith did not penetrate beyond the shadow that Satan had cast athwart their horizon.[5]

What a difference a day makes. By Sunday night, one week after the triumphal entry, the disciples once again were on an emotional high. Only this time, their cause for rejoicing was grounded in God's unfolding plan for the salvation of human beings and not upon preconceived human opinions. Jesus had been raised from the dead, and He had appeared to His followers. Now they saw everything from a different perspective. As Peter testifies, God "hath begotten us again unto a lively [living] hope by the resurrection of Jesus Christ from the dead" (1 Peter 1:3).

Living Hope

What is the nature of this living hope that now fills Peter's heart with such joy and exuberance—this hope to which God has begotten all who place their faith in the resurrected Jesus? The apostle describes it in verses 4 and 5 as "an inheritance incorruptible, and undefiled, and that fadeth not away, reserved in heaven for you, who are kept by the power of God through faith unto salvation ready to be revealed in the last time."

How much more glorious was Peter's hope after the resurrection than before. Before the resurrection, his hope had centered in an earthly kingdom and in the restored glory of national Israel. After the resurrection, his hope centered in an eternal kingdom, eternal life, the earth made new, and an incorruptible inheritance. "Thus the death of Christ—the very event which the disciples had looked upon as the final destruction of their hope—was that which made it forever sure."[6]

Being a natural descendant of Abraham, Peter was interested in the inheritance outlined in the covenant promises that God gave to his ancestor. But following the resurrection of Jesus, he had a new slant on this inheritance. Not to be realized within this world of sin, it is an incorruptible inheritance, one that is undefiled and does not fade away, reserved in heaven for all who believe.

When Jesus and John the Baptist began their ministries, it was popularly believed that all of Abraham's children were guaranteed an inheritance in the Messiah's kingdom. John warned his listeners not to put their trust in this popular idea: "Begin not to say within yourselves, We have Abraham to our father: for I say unto you, That God is able of these stones to raise up children unto Abraham" (Luke 3:8).

Paul acknowledged advantages to being a Jew (Romans 3:2; 9:4, 5), but these advantages do not include a guarantee of salvation: "For they are not all Israel, which are of Israel: neither, because they are the seed of Abraham, are they all children: but, In Isaac shall thy seed be called" (Romans 9:6, 7).

One of the great truths running through the New Testament is that the kingdom of Christ is open to anyone who believes. The covenant promise that all the nations would be blessed in Abraham (Galatians 3:8) is seen as fulfilled in Christ: "Now the promises were made to Abraham and to his offspring. It does not say, 'And to offsprings,' referring to many; but, referring to one, 'And to your offspring,' which is Christ" (Galatians 3:16, RSV). Because the promises made to Abraham are realized in Christ, He, in turn, shares them with anyone who accepts Him in faith.

Thus all nations, Jew or Gentile, may share in the inheritance. As the apostle Paul states:

> Ye are all the children of God by faith in Christ Jesus. For as many of you as have been baptized into Christ have put on Christ. There is neither Jew nor Greek, there is neither bond nor free, there is neither male or female: for ye are all one in Christ Jesus. And if ye be Christ's, then are ye Abraham's seed, and heirs according to the promise (Galatians 3:26-29).

What a difference exists between the living hope that has been made possible by the resurrection of Jesus and what the world has to offer: "The treasure we are seeking is imperishable, eternal, immortal, all overglorious; while that of which the worldling is in pursuit, endures but a day; it is fading, perishable, fleeting as the morning cloud."[7]

Kept by the Power of God

Now we begin to understand the reasons for Peter's optimism. We are not only begotten again to a living hope, to an inheritance that far surpasses anything we can imagine, but we are guarded by God day by day as we encounter difficulties resulting from Adam's sin. How encouraging are the words of Ellen White: "Nothing in this world is so dear to God as His church; nothing is guarded by Him with such jealous care; nothing so offends Him as when injury is inflicted on His servants and His church."[8]

The question naturally arises, From what does God guard His people? Does He keep them at all times from physical harm? We would have to answer No! For we have known

OUR LIVING HOPE 31

sincere Christians who have suffered from illness or accidents. Ellen White recognizes that God's people will suffer physically when she says, "When injury is inflicted on His servants," God is offended. From what, then, does God guard His people? From emotional harm, from mental abuse, or from character assassination? Again we would have to say No! For we have known true people of God who have suffered all of these—and other abuses.

First Peter 1:5 clearly states why God guards His people and alludes to that from which we are protected. They "are kept by the power of God through faith *unto salvation* ready to be revealed in the last time." God sets a guard around His people as they fight the battle against sin and the powers of evil. It is not God's will that they be swept away by the forces of the enemy into gloom and eternal destruction. They are His trophies in the great controversy, His jewels purchased by the blood of Christ, His lights in a sea of darkness. They may be abused and persecuted by those who hate truth, they may suffer for their faith, but no power on earth or in hell will snatch them from the hand of their God as long as they are faithful and true. As His treasures, they will glorify and vindicate Him before the world and the universe as He reveals the final saving acts at the end of the controversy.

> The believers in the truth are guarded jealously as the heart of God. In the fierce conflict before us, mind with mind, truth in collision with error, principle with principle, this world will witness scenes that are intensely interesting, of immense importance.[9]

> We are not kept by our intelligence, by our words, or by our riches. In these we find no safety. We are kept only by the power of God through faith unto salvation. We are living in a period of time during which we must by faith be allied with an infinite God, or else we cannot overcome the strong powers of darkness seeking to destroy us. The Holy Spirit is as a light shining on our pathway. Let us put our trust in Christ, who is ever at

our right hand to help us. Let us take courage, placing our confidence and our trust in Him. He has not left us destitute.[10]

The guard around each believer is maintained upon conditions. The first—faith—is stressed in verse 5. Ellen White emphasizes this condition in the quotation above, "Let us put our trust in Christ." As long as this faith and trust is maintained, we have the assurance that a guard has been posted around us, and that Satan cannot pull us down to eternal destruction.

For this reason the enemy of our souls works tirelessly to break our trust in Christ. Our work is to keep our faith and trust constant. This responsibility God has given to us, and He will not do for us what He requires on our part in the battle against sin.

> Trust in its fullness comes to us through constant communion with God. By eating the flesh and drinking the blood of Christ we gain spiritual strength. Christ supplies the lifeblood of the heart, and Christ and the Holy Spirit give nerve power. Begotten again unto a lively hope, imbued with the quickening power of a new nature, the soul is enabled to rise higher and still higher.[11]

Another condition upon which God maintains guards around His people is obedience.

> All who obey God's commandments are kept by His mighty power amid the corrupting influence of the transgressors of His law. From the lowliest subject to the highest in positions of trust, they are kept by the power of God through faith unto salvation.[12]

Trust and obey, and the mighty forces of heaven engulf the humble children of God. Even when they are despised and abused by the world, no one can eternally hurt or destroy

OUR LIVING HOPE 33

them. As long as they choose to keep on trusting and obeying, they dwell in the secret places of the Most High and abide under the shadow of the Almighty.

Summary

The promise is to those who will put their faith and trust in Jesus, to those who have committed themselves to obedience because they love Him. He will keep them in the hollow of His hand: He will grant them peace because their minds are stayed upon Him. Satan cannot take them away from the Saviour as long as they choose to maintain their relationship with Him, and all heaven is committed to help each child of God to strengthen that relationship. Peter's excitement and joy over the future is ours as well. Jesus, in cooperation with His Father and the Holy Spirit, has done so much for us, we cannot help but join Peter in praise: "Blessed be the God and Father of our Lord Jesus Christ, which according to his abundant mercy hath begotten us again unto a lively hope by the resurrection of Jesus Christ from the dead" (verse 3).

---

1. *The Desire of Ages*, p. 570.
2. Ibid., p. 590.
3. Ibid., p. 593.
4. *The Great Controversy*, pp. 348, 349.
5. *The Acts of the Apostles*, p. 26.
6. *The Great Controversy*, p. 348.
7. *Testimonies for the Church*, vol. 2, p. 47.
8. Letter 19, 1901.
9. Manuscript 6, 1894.
10. *Notebook Leaflets*, vol. 1, no. 16, p. 4.
11. *Counsels on Health*, p. 593.
12. *Evangelism*, p. 316.

Chapter 4
The Triumph of Faith

1 Peter 1:6-12

Have you ever heard of the "worm" syndrome? If you haven't, let me identify it for you. This syndrome is an incorrect application of biblical passages that speak of the lowliness of human beings. This biblical concept has been put into the words of a hymn, and we sing "such a worm as I." David says, "I am a worm, and no man" (Psalm 22:6), and God said to Israel, "Fear not, thou worm Jacob, and ye men of Israel" (Isaiah 41:14).

Our low estate, resulting from the entrance of sin, is a biblical concept, but some Christians misapply it. They seem to think that they lack spiritual excellence unless their social relations are structured upon their "worminess." The pathetic image they project does not witness to the glory of their Creator and Redeemer. Thus the "worm" syndrome. We must realize that God wants a healthy balance in Christian humility. First, we will readily recognize that we are human—the sons and daughters of Adam, "carnal, sold under sin" (Romans 7:14). Next we will admit and confess the presence and reality of sin within the life, humbling ourselves in the presence of

Jesus as we admit and accept the striking contrast between sinner and Redeemer.

Ellen White describes healthy humility this way:

> Many see much to admire in the life of Christ. But true love for Him can never dwell in the heart of the self-righteous. Not to see our own deformity is not to see the beauty of Christ's character. When we are fully awake to our own sinfulness, we shall appreciate Christ. The more humble are our views of ourselves, the more clearly we shall see the spotless character of Jesus. . . . Not to see the marked contrast between Christ and ourselves is not to know ourselves. He who does not abhor himself cannot understand the meaning of redemption.[1]

Ellen White's words "He who does not abhor himself" do not describe the "worm" syndrome. Rather, she is talking about a genuine experience in redemption. She wants Christians to understand that we are defiled by sin and to be willing to admit it, but also to understand that God has provided a means of cleansing—the precious blood of Jesus. Having been washed in the blood of the Lamb, self-confessed sinners can rejoice in their new identity as children of God.

As a sinner, when I look upon the spotless character of Jesus, I am undone; but as I look upon the cross, I see the value God places upon me. When I can admit to myself and to God that I am but a child of Adam, I lie broken on the Rock. At this point God can begin to repair the damage caused by sin. As my understanding of God's saving plan grows, my faith grows; and I glory in the fact that God has begotten me again to a living hope, to an inheritance that is imperishable, undefiled, unfading, and kept in heaven while I am guarded here on earth. In this I rejoice.

Then, as I endure trials, the quality of my faith in God will be seen. Peter compares the faith of God's people with gold. Human beings establish the value of gold, but God establishes the value of genuine faith. The One who placed gold ore in the earth says faith is of more value than the purest gold that a furnace can refine, because it is my faith that will "redound to praise and glory and honor at the revelation of Jesus Christ" (1 Peter 1:7, RSV).

> Those who hold fast their faith unto the end will come forth from the furnace of trial as fine gold seven times purified. Of this work the prophet Isaiah says, "I will make a man more precious than fine gold; even a man than the golden wedge of Ophir" (Isaiah 13:12). When in trouble, remember that faith tried in the furnace of affliction is more precious than gold tried with fire. Remember that there is One watching every movement, to see when the last particle of dross is taken away from your character.[2]

So my position ("such a worm as I") in this world of sin, which is the result of my descent from Adam, must be placed beside the cross of Jesus in order to preserve a balance. Although I am a sinner, my value in the eyes of my Creator and the value of my faith in Him far exceeds the most precious material treasures.

Apostle From Missouri

Recalling an experience one night in the upper room, Peter gives another reason why God treasures the faith of His people: "Whom having not seen, ye love; in whom, though now ye see him not, yet believing, ye rejoice with joy unspeakable and full of glory: Receiving the end of your faith, even the salvation of your souls" (verses 8, 9).

Peter has in mind the experience of Thomas, who missed the first post-resurrection appearance of Jesus. Although the other apostles tried to convince Thomas that Jesus had indeed risen from the dead, he refused to believe their report:

> Except I shall see in his hands the print of the nails, and put my finger into the print of the nails, and thrust my hand into his side, I will not believe.

And after eight days again his disciples were within, and Thomas with them: then came Jesus, the doors being shut, and stood in the midst, and said, Peace be unto you. Then saith he to Thomas, Reach hither thy finger, and behold my hands; and reach hither thy hand, and thrust it into my side: and be not faithless, but believing. And Thomas answered and said unto him, My Lord and my God. Jesus saith unto him, Thomas, because thou hast seen me, thou hast believed: blessed are they that have not seen, and yet have believed (John 20:25-29).

Thomas had abundant opportunity to believe. Consider the evidence that faced him during the week that separated the first two appearances to the apostles. First, Jesus appeared to Mary that resurrection morning as she lingered at the empty tomb. She, in turn, went back to the city and reported the appearance to the apostles (John 20:11-18).

Mary originally went to the tomb with a group of women who were disciples of Jesus. Upon seeing the angels in the tomb and receiving instructions to report to the apostles that Jesus had risen, the women went to find the apostles while Mary stayed behind. After appearing to Mary, Jesus then intercepted the group of women and made Himself known to them (Matthew 28:9, 10).

It is interesting that as Mary and the women reported to the apostles these two appearances of Jesus, "Their words seemed to them as idle tales, and they believed them not" (Luke 24:11). So for several hours on resurrection Sunday, all of the apostles were behaving as though they were from Missouri, but poor Thomas was the one who got stuck with the label—"doubter."

The third appearance that day was, as far as we can tell, to Peter (1 Corinthians 15:5). Then Jesus walked to Emmaus with Cleopas and his companion (Luke 24:13-35). Accepting the invitation of hospitality, Jesus made Himself known by the breaking of bread. After He disappeared, the two disciples retraced their steps to Jerusalem, eager to confirm the earlier

THE TRIUMPH OF FAITH   39

reports of the women. They found that Jesus' appearance to Peter was the subject of conversation and rejoicing. Everyone present was now a believer.

While the upper room was abuzz over these exciting experiences, Jesus appeared to the entire group (Luke 24:36-48). From this fifth appearance (but first to the apostolic group) in less than twenty-four hours after the resurrection, Thomas was missing. It may very well be that before the week was out, Jesus also appeared to His brother James (1 Corinthians 15:7).

For an entire week Thomas listened to repeated reports of the appearances but sulked in the gloom of doubt. Notice that when Jesus finally confronted Thomas, He gave him neither harsh rebuke nor condemnation. Jesus simply furnished the evidence that Thomas demanded and waited for faith to grow under the impressions of the Holy Spirit.

> In His treatment of Thomas, Jesus gave a lesson for His followers. His example shows how we should treat those whose faith is weak, and who make their doubts prominent. Jesus did not overwhelm Thomas with reproach, nor did He enter into controversy with him. He revealed Himself to the doubting one. Thomas had been most unreasonable in dictating the conditions of his faith, but Jesus, by His generous love and consideration, broke down all the barriers. Unbelief is seldom overcome by controversy. It is rather put upon self-defense, and finds new support and excuse. But let Jesus, in His love and mercy, be revealed as the crucified Saviour, and from many once unwilling lips will be heard the acknowledgment of Thomas. "My Lord and my God."[3]

In alluding to Thomas's experience, Peter speaks to us. We have not seen Jesus, yet we love Him and believe in Him. From His words to Thomas, we know that our faith and trust please Him. We also know He exists because we can see tangible results from our relationship with Him. Therefore, we can rejoice in Him "with unutterable and exalted joy" (1 Peter

1:8, RSV) whatever our present situation may be, and look to the future with confidence because we know He has redeemed us.

As Peter penned the following words, "Whom having not seen, ye love; in whom, though now ye see him not, yet believing" (verse 8), he compared the experience of Thomas with the genuine love his readers had for Jesus, whom they had never seen. He perhaps also mused over the contrast between their faith, based only on a verbal report, and his unbelief when confronted with the empty tomb on resurrection morning.

Mystery of the Cross

If the reader of the Bible misses the great controversy theme, many things taught in its sacred pages will seem to be disjointed, disconnected ideas. Understanding the great controversy between good and evil helps the pieces in the great mosaic fall into place and the messages of the Old and New Testaments take on their proper meaning.

In connection with understanding the great controversy, Peter introduces an interesting insight. The men whom God chose to write the Old Testament books did not fully understand the revelations committed to them. "The meaning" of the plan of redemption about which the Holy Spirit inspired them to write, "was to be unfolded from age to age, as the people of God should need the instruction therein contained."[4]

This delayed clarification did not stop them from searching for answers to questions that intrigued them. For example, the revelation that the Messiah was to suffer concerned them deeply. They wanted to know more about His life, the time when He was to suffer, the reasons why He had to suffer, and the circumstances under which He would suffer. Jesus told His followers, "Verily I say unto you, That many prophets and righteous men have desired to see those things which ye see, and have not seen them; and to hear those things which ye hear, and have not heard them" (Matthew 13:17). The writers were told that what they were inspired to write was not for their edification but for the generations that were to follow (1 Peter 1:10-12).

To impress the reader with the depth of interest in the plan of redemption, Peter intensifies both Greek verbs in verse 10—*searched* and *inquired*—by adding prepositions. The sentence structure suggests this meaning: the prophets diligently sought and carefully inquired after an understanding of God's plan for humanity.

Ellen White expands upon Peter's thought and tells us that the study of the theme of salvation is the highest study in which we can engage:

> The science of redemption is the science of all sciences, the science that is the study of the angels and of all the intelligences of the unfallen worlds, the science that engages the attention of our Lord and Saviour, the science that enters into the purpose brooded in the mind of the Infinite—"kept in silence through times eternal," the science that will be the study of God's redeemed throughout the endless ages. This is the highest study in which it is possible for man to engage. As no other study can, it will quicken the mind and uplift the soul.[5]

The Old Testament prophets are not alone in their desire to know more fully God's plan for dealing with sin. Even the angels need to understand more clearly the experience of sin and redemption. Because they fought at Jesus' side in the beginning of the great controversy and are now active participants in its closing scenes, they feel closely tied to all of the events of the cosmic drama. They, too, long to look into the mysteries of redemption.

> It had been difficult even for the angels to grasp the mystery of redemption—to comprehend that the Commander of heaven, the Son of God, must die for guilty man. When the command was given to Abraham to offer up his son, the interest of all heavenly beings was enlisted. With intense earnestness they watched each step in the fulfillment of this command. When to Isaac's ques-

tion, "Where is the lamb for a burnt offering?" Abraham made answer, "God will provide Himself a lamb;" and when the father's hand was stayed as he was about to slay his son, and the ram which God had provided was offered in the place of Isaac—then light was shed upon the mystery of redemption, and even the angels understood more clearly the wonderful provision that God had made for man's salvation.[6]

An additional mystery to the angels was "how Christ could live and work in a fallen world, how He could mingle with sinful humanity. It was a mystery to them that He who hated sin with intense hatred felt the most tender, compassionate sympathy for the beings that committed sin."[7]

Summary

A healthy Christian will keep a balance between an acknowledgment of his sinful condition, his recognized need for Jesus' grace and forgiveness, and the assurance that his sins are forgiven and he is accepted in Jesus. This balanced perspective can be maintained only as the sinner spends time with his Lord in study and prayer. As his spiritual sight becomes clearer, he sees as never before the loveliness and purity of Jesus. Although the physical eye has not beheld Him, the eye of faith, having been anointed with the eye salve of the Spirit, is keen and sharp. As a result, the Christian loves Him whom they have not seen, and God is pleased.

But because their understanding of what heaven paid for their salvation is incomplete, they join prophets and angels in the study that will occupy their attention and interest through the ceaseless ages of eternity.

---

1. "Self-Exaltation," *The Advent Review and Sabbath Herald,* September 25, 1900.
2. *The Upward Look,* p. 292.

3. *The Desire of Ages,* p. 808.
4. *The Great Controversy*, p. 344.
5. *My Life Today*, p. 360.
6. *Patriarchs and Prophets*, p. 155.
7. "The Way, The Truth, and The Life," *Signs of the Times*, January 20, 1898.

Chapter 5
Call to Holy Living

1 Peter 1:13-25

Can sinful people be holy? Some think they are, and they are not bashful in telling you so. The description of the Laodicean church summarizes God's view of people who perceive themselves as holy. They see themselves as "rich, and increased with goods, and [in] need of nothing." But Jesus evaluates their spiritual condition differently: They are "wretched, and miserable, and poor, and blind, and naked" (Revelation 3:17).

Ellen White puts her finger on the underlying cause of the Laodicean problem of self-righteousness:

> The claim to be without sin is, in itself, evidence that he who makes this claim is far from holy. It is because he has no true conception of the infinite purity and holiness of God or of what they must become who shall be in harmony with His character; because he has no true conception of the purity and exalted loveliness of Jesus, and the malignity and evil of sin, that man can regard himself as holy. The greater the distance between himself and Christ, and the more inadequate his conceptions of

the divine character and requirements, the more righteous he appears in his own eyes.[1]

She identifies three causes of a self-righteous attitude: a failure to (1) see and understand the purity and holiness of God; (2) understand what God wants us to become under His transforming grace; and (3) understand the malignity of sin and how offensive it is to God. These three may be summarized in this statement: "The greater the distance between himself and Christ . . . the more righteous he appears in his own eyes."

The attitude of the Pharisee in Jesus' parable who went into the temple to pray suggests that he would have been a highly respected member in the Laodicean church: "God, I thank thee, that I am not as other men are, . . . I fast twice in the week, I give tithes of all that I possess," he said (Luke 18:11, 12). Concerning this man, Ellen White says, "The Pharisee's boastful, self-righteous prayer showed that his heart was closed against the influence of the Holy Spirit. Because of his distance from God, he had no sense of his own defilement, in contrast with the perfection of the divine holiness. He felt no need, and he received nothing."[2]

Call to Holiness

Holiness is an imperative, something God requires of us. Throughout 1 Peter 1:13-16, Peter calls his readers to nobler and holier Christian living in a variety of ways. Each call is expressed with some form of an imperative (command). For example, Peter uses: (1) two imperative participles ("gird up" and "be sober," verse 13); (2) a prohibitive imperative participle ("not fashioning"—KJV, or "do not be conformed"—RSV, verse 14); (3) two imperative verbs ("hope," verse 13 and "be holy," verse 15); and (4) an future imperative verb ("be ye holy"—KJV, or "you shall be holy"—RSV, verse 16).

It's difficult to imagine how Peter could be any clearer. Speaking on behalf of God, the apostle is calling all Christians to holy living, to lives that are separated from the folly and sin that occupy the energy, interests, time, and money of those who know not God. Quoting God's instruction from the book of Leviticus, Peter writes, "Be ye holy; for I am holy" (verse 16).

Because He is without sin, God alone possesses holiness as a part of His nature. Holiness, as an attribute possessed by Jesus, was present when He was born into the world. When Gabriel announced the incarnation to Mary, he said, "Therefore also that holy thing which shall be born of thee shall be called the Son of God" (Luke 1:35). Commenting on this verse, Ellen White says, "The humanity of Christ is called 'that holy thing.' "[3] This statement reflects two penetrating insights regarding the nature of Jesus: (1) He did indeed take our humanity ("except without the taint of sin"[4]), and (2) Jesus' "spiritual nature was free from every taint of sin."[5]

This, however, is not the case with human beings, for no one receives holiness as a birthright or as a gift passed from one human being to another.[6] Jesus received a human body from His mother, Mary, and a sinless spiritual nature from His Father. Thus it is that Jesus could be called "that holy thing" by Gabriel.

We, however, are sinful and evil by nature. Paul says to the Ephesians, "We were by nature children of wrath, like the rest of mankind" (Ephesians 2:3, RSV). Ellen White says, "The result of the eating of the tree of knowledge of good and evil is manifest in every man's experience. There is in his nature a bent to evil, a force which, unaided, he cannot resist."[7] She also says, "At its very source human nature was corrupted."[8] Yet God calls His children to holiness.

The holiness that God possesses as a natural attribute human beings do not possess. However, when a sinner surrenders his life to Jesus, holiness is given to him as a gift: "Holiness is the gift of God through Christ. Those who receive the Saviour become sons of God. They are His spiritual children, born again, renewed in righteousness and true holiness."[9] At the time of the new birth, the heart is brought into harmony with God and His law. When this happens, the sinner passes from death to life, from sin to holiness.[10]

God is calling His people to a standard of living that is consistent with the requirements of His Word and that reflects the character of Jesus. This goal is achieved only through the power of the indwelling Spirit. The fruit produced in the life gives evidence that the believer has received the gift of holiness.

> The truths of the Word of God meet in one grand practical necessity—the conversion of the soul through faith. When the believer is united with Christ, that faith is manifested in holiness of character, in consistent obedience to every word that proceedeth out of the mouth of God. The grand principles of the Word of God are not to be thought too pure and holy to be brought into the daily life. The truths of the Word of God are truths which reach to heaven and compass eternity; and yet their vital influence is to be woven into the human life. The influence of the Word of God is to have a sanctifying effect on our speech, our actions, our associations with every member of the human family. It must bring under its control the temper and the voice. The apostle exhorts us: "As He which hath called you is holy, so be ye holy in all manner of conversation; because it is written, Be ye holy; for I am holy."[11]

Victorious Living

Peter's call to holiness is a recognition that such a state can be achieved only by washing in the blood of Christ, being filled with the Spirit of Christ, and living a life obedient to the will of God. Many who call themselves Christians herald forgiveness of sin and justification by faith, but say little about an obedient life. Peter calls his readers to a new lifestyle: "As obedient children, do not be conformed to the passions of your former ignorance, but as he who called you is holy, be holy yourselves in all your conduct; since it is written, 'You shall be holy, for I am holy'" (1 Peter 1:14-16, RSV). Peter is talking in terms of victory over sin.

To understand what God desires of us as He calls us to holiness, the following points are set forth. We must: (1) admit our own sinfulness, (2) recognize that God expects us to be victori-

CALL TO HOLY LIVING 49

ous over besetting sin, and (3) be aware of how victory is gained.

Admit our sinfulness. Paul makes it clear that all of us are under the curse of sin as a result of Adam's fall: "Wherefore, as by one man sin entered into the world, and death by sin; and so death passed upon all men, for that all have sinned" (Romans 5:12). Through disobedience Adam fell "from a state of perfect happiness to a state of misery and sin."[12] As a result, all of his descendants are born into this world in a state of sin, a state of rebellion and alienation from God. Each is born with a fallen human nature that is bent toward evil.

Ellen White shares an interesting insight when she compares Seth and Cain:

> Seth was of more noble stature than Cain or Abel, and resembled Adam more closely than did his other sons. He was a worthy character, following in the steps of Abel. Yet he inherited no more natural goodness than did Cain. Concerning the creation of Adam it is said, "In the likeness of God made He him"; but man, after the Fall "begat a son in his *own* likeness, after *his* image." While Adam was created sinless, in the likeness of God, Seth, like Cain, inherited the fallen nature of his parents.[13]

None have escaped the consequences of Adam's choice—sin and death. Paul emphasizes this fact when he says, "What then? are we better than they? No, in no wise: for we have before proved both Jew and Gentiles, that they are all under sin" (Romans 3:9). He stresses his point again by saying, "God has consigned all men to disobedience" (Romans 11:32, RSV), and "the scripture hath concluded all under sin" (Galatians 3:22).

An important step in victory over sin is a willingness to recognize that, as Adam's children, we have been born into a state of sin which is seen (1) in the bent that we all possess toward disobedience and (2) by the acts of sin we commit. We cannot change our sinful natures; we cannot of ourselves change the direction in which we are headed at birth. Only Jesus and the power of His Spirit can accomplish that. When we admit to ourselves and to God the reality of our sinful natures, we take a big step in the direction of holiness.

Victory over sin. The New Testament clearly teaches that victory over sin is essential for every follower of Jesus. The apostle Paul says, "Let not sin therefore reign in your mortal body, that ye should obey it in the lusts thereof. . . . For sin shall not have dominion over you: for ye are not under the law, but under grace" (Romans 6:12-14). He also says to the Corinthians, "Awake to righteousness, and sin not" (1 Corinthians 15:34); and to the Galatians, "But I say, walk by the Spirit, and do not gratify the desires of the flesh. For the desires of the flesh are against the Spirit, and the desires of the Spirit are against the flesh; for these are opposed to each other, to prevent you from doing what you would." "And those who belong to Christ Jesus have crucified the flesh with its passions and desires" (Galatians 5:16, 17, 24, RSV).

The Hebrew Christians are admonished to lay aside every weight and the sin that besets them (Hebrews 12:1). But perhaps the beloved disciple John is the clearest of all New Testament writers: "Whosoever abideth in him sinneth not: whosoever sinneth hath not seen him, neither known him. . . . Whosoever is born of God doth not commit sin; for his seed remaineth in him: and he cannot sin, because he is born of God" (1 John 3:6-9).

Peter himself says that we are dead to sins; therefore, we should live to righteousness (1 Peter 2:24). He also says that we are to give diligence to make our calling and election sure. If we do that, we will never fall (2 Peter 1:10).

Repeatedly the New Testament writers instruct their readers to lay aside the lusts and passions of the flesh, calling upon them to turn from sin in all of its forms. For example, Peter says, "Dearly beloved, I beseech you as strangers and pilgrims, abstain from fleshly lusts, which war against the soul" (1 Peter 2:11). And Paul says, "The night is far spent, the day is at hand: let us therefore cast off the works of darkness, and let us put on the armour of light. . . . But put ye on the Lord Jesus Christ, and make not provision for the flesh, to fulfil the lusts thereof" (Romans 13:12-14).

Paul tells his Roman readers to present their bodies to God as a living sacrifice, holy and acceptable (see Romans 12:1). Every sacrifice offered to God in the sanctuary service was without spot or blemish. This same high standard Paul has in mind for all Christians—they are to be holy and without blemish.

Ellen White adds her voice to those of the New Testament writers: "He who has not sufficient faith in Christ to believe that He can keep him from sinning, has not the faith that will give him an entrance into the kingdom of God."[14] Again she says, "Do you suppose that after Christ gave His precious life to redeem the beings He created, He would fail to give them sufficient power to enable them to overcome by the blood of the Lamb and the word of their testimony? He has power to save every individual."[15]

Although the New Testament holds out the joy of victory over sin, this will not lead the children of God into triumphalism, nor into the trap of perfectionism. For every disciple who speaks so strongly about victory over sin also says, "If we say we have no sin, we deceive ourselves, and the truth is not in us. . . . If we say we have not sinned, we make him a liar, and his word is not in us" (1 John 1:8-10).

Victory over sin is ours as we link our wills with the power of the Spirit of Jesus. But the closer we come to Jesus, the more defiled we appear in our own eyes, even though God is giving us victory over besetting sins. Therefore, there is no room for boasting, spiritual triumphalism, or perfectionism. Ellen White describes the growing Christian's self-perception this way:

> We may have flattered ourselves, as did Nicodemus, that our life has been upright, that our moral character is correct, and think that we need not humble the heart before God, like the common sinner: but when the light from Christ shines into our souls, we shall see how impure we are; we shall discern the selfishness of motive, the enmity against God, that has defiled every act of life. Then we shall know that our own righteousness is indeed

as filthy rags, and that the blood of Christ alone can cleanse us from the defilement of sin, and renew our hearts in His own likeness.[16]

Steps to victory. The first step to victory over sin is admitting to ourselves and to God that we are sinners, that by nature we are evil, and that we possess a fallen sin-nature. With this admission, the next step is possible—the surrender of self, of all, to the will of God.[17] This is the right exercise of the will.[18]

When we take the second step, two things happen: (1) the fallen nature is "brought under the control of the Spirit of Christ,"[19] and (2) the human will is merged with the will of God.[20] This now prepares the way for the third step and victory over sin:

> The expulsion of sin is the act of the soul itself. True, we have no power to free ourselves from Satan's control; but when we desire to be set free from sin, and in our great need cry out for a power out of and above ourselves, the powers of the soul are imbued with the divine energy of the Holy Spirit, and they obey the dictates of the will in fulfilling the will of God.[21]

As the Holy Spirit takes control of the fallen nature, He energizes the powers of our spiritual nature. The human will, which becomes an extension of God's will at the time of surrender, dictates to the powers of the human spiritual nature: and these powers, which are imbued with the divine power of the Spirit, jettison sinful practices out of the life. The entire experience is a working relationship between the sinner and the Holy Spirit. The Spirit supplies the power, the sinner supplies the will, and victory over sin is the result.

Although the Spirit controls the fallen sin-nature, He does not remove it. This nature is a part of us and will be with us until Jesus returns and "this corruptible shall have put on incorruption, and this mortal shall have put on immortality" (1 Corinthians 15:54). For this reason, New Testament writers instruct Christians to turn away from the former lifestyle that gratified the desires and passions of the flesh. Paul says, "Finally, brethren, whatsoever things are true, whatsoever things are honest, whatsoever things are just, whatsoever things are pure, whatsoever things are lovely, whatsoever things are of good report; if there be any virtue, and if there be any praise, think on these things" (Philippians 4:8).

Peter admonishes Christians to live, "As obedient children, not fashioning yourselves according to the former lusts in your ignorance" (1 Peter 1:14). And Ellen White says:

> The apostle [Peter] sought to teach the believers how important it is to keep the mind from wandering to forbidden themes or from spending its energies on trifling subjects. Those who would not fall a prey to Satan's devices, must guard well the avenues of the soul; they must avoid reading, seeing, or hearing that which will suggest impure thoughts. The mind must not be left to dwell at random upon every subject that the enemy of souls may suggest. The heart must be faithfully sentineled, or *evils without will awaken evils within, and the soul will wander in darkness.*[22]

Summary

The born-again child of God is given the gift of holiness. This state of spiritual existence is maintained by: (1) the Holy Spirit's controlling the fallen sin-nature that we all possess, (2) the powers of the spiritual nature obeying the human will, which has become an extension of God's will, and jettisoning sinful habits and practices, and (3) the avenues to the soul being guarded so that evils without cannot awaken evils within. Thus victory over sin and resting in the gift of holiness are available to all.

---

1. *The Great Controversy*, p. 473.
2. *Steps to Christ*, p. 31.
3. "Sin Condemned in the Flesh," *Signs of the Times*, January 16, 1896.

4. Manuscript Release 1211.
5. *Seventh-day Adventist Bible Commentary*, vol. 5, p. 1104.
6. Ibid., vol. 6, p. 1117.
7. *Education*, p. 29.
8. "The Warfare Between Good and Evil," *The Adventist Review and Sabbath Herald*, April 16, 1901.
9. *Seventh-day Adventist Bible Commentary*, vol. 6, p. 1117.
10. *The Great Controversy*, p. 468.
11. "The Power of the Truth in the Daily Life," *Signs of the Times*, October 27, 1898.
12. *Spiritual Gifts*, vol. 3, p. 58.
13. *Patriarchs and Prophets*, p. 80.
14. *Selected Messages*, bk. 3, p. 360.
15. Manuscript 110, 1901.
16. *Steps to Christ*, pp. 28, 29.
17. Ibid., p. 43.
18. Ibid., p. 47.
19. Ibid.
20. *Christ's Object Lessons*, p. 312.
21. *The Desire of Ages*, p. 466.
22. *The Acts of the Apostles*, p. 518, emphasis supplied.

Chapter 6
God's Showcase

1 Peter 2:1-10

When I opened the door I was surprised; for some reason I expected someone much younger. But they were an attractive couple somewhere in their middle sixties. We had advertised a two-manual organ for sale in the local newspaper, and this Mormon couple had stopped by to look at it. After we led them into the living room, the woman slipped onto the bench, turned the organ on, and began to play from memory the hymn that has become identified with the Mormon Church, "Come, Come Ye Saints." Turning to my wife, she said with firm conviction, "That's us, you know."

There was a time when the members of each Christian denomination firmly believed that they were God's saints, God's chosen people. For various reasons, people in other denominations did not quite qualify for the honor. If, however, a member came to believe that his denomination no longer held the honor of being the people of God, he would surely begin a search to find the true church; and when he found it, he would join it.

It seems that ecumenism has, to a great degree, changed all this. A spirit of "Christian love" is in the air, a tolerance for others' religious persuasions. The entire Christian community, encompassing various denominations and beliefs, are considered to be God's people. Doctrinal beliefs no longer separate people into believers and nonbelievers. It no longer even matters what your doctrinal position is. Baptism by sprinkling, for example, is as acceptable as baptism by immersion, variations in lifestyle are not as important as they used to be, differences in prophetic interpretation and in ideas relating to the second advent of Jesus and the end of the world scarcely cause a ripple.

Only among the few denominations holding to unique beliefs do you still find the old idea "We are the chosen people of God"—as among the Mormons, Jehovah's Witnesses, and Seventh-day Adventists. (Even among these churches self-identification is weakening.) But is this wrong? Is it wrong to take a stand with a group of people that holds to unique doctrinal beliefs because you are convicted that these beliefs accurately represent biblical truth? The writers of the New Testament would not consider it to be wrong, for this is exactly what they did.

God's People

From Abraham in the book of Genesis to the end of Revelation, the Bible presents the concept of a chosen people. As Moses reviewed the experience of Israel, he said, "Thou art an holy people unto the Lord thy God: the Lord thy God hath chosen thee to be a special people unto himself, above all people that are upon the face of the earth" (Deuteronomy 7:6). This biblical concept of chosenness runs throughout the Old Testament.

The theme continues in the New Testament—only with a new emphasis. Those originally chosen disqualified themselves for the honor of being "the people" because they rejected the One who gives the people reason for existing. God's people now find their identity in Jesus:

> For as many of you as have been baptized into Christ have put on Christ. There is neither Jew nor Greek, there is neither bond nor free, there is neither male nor female: for ye are all one in Christ Jesus. And if ye be

Christ's, then are ye Abraham's seed, and heirs according to the promise (Galatians 3:26-29).

New Israel is now composed of all who believe in Jesus, both Jews and Gentiles. The unique doctrinal belief that Jesus is the Messiah, the Son of God, identified the early Christians as God's people. But then, the New Testament introduces us to an interesting phenomenon. The time would come when not all who claim to be Christians—followers of Christ—would be God's people.

The apostle Paul warned the Ephesian elders, "I know this, that after my departing shall grievous wolves enter in among you, not sparing the flock. Also of your own selves shall men arise, speaking perverse things, to draw away disciples after them" (Acts 20:29, 30). To the Christians in Thessalonica Paul wrote, "Let no man deceive you by any means: for that day shall not come, except there come a falling away first, and that man of sin be revealed, the son of perdition." "Even him, whose coming is after the working of Satan with all power and signs and lying wonders, and with all deceivableness of unrighteousness in them that perish; because they received not the love of the truth, that they might be saved" (2 Thessalonians 2:3, 9, 10).

It is the product of this falling away from truth that John identifies in Revelation as the beast (13:1-10), the harlot (17:1-6), and Babylon (14:8; 18:1-24). As the end of time approaches, a great cry goes out to the four corners of the earth for God's people who are still in Babylon to leave it (14:8) so they will not receive the punishment that is about to be inflicted upon her (18:1-4). Responding to the call, they join forces with those who are sounding the warning and who are identified by their doctrinal position—keeping the commandments of God and having the testimony and faith that comes from Jesus (12:17; 14:12).

Ecumenism has blurred the distinctness of many Christian bodies. Their doctrinal positions merge, blur, and then fade. They lack the clear, crisp marks of identification as presented in Revelation 12:17 and 14:12. Even the unique beliefs that separate several denominations from the main body of Christians do not qualify them as God's end-time people, according to the criteria of Revelation.

Only the Seventh-day Adventist Church meets the qualifications of Revelation 12:17 and 14:12.

A Holy Nation

Peter's assessment of Christ's church is another example of his enthusiasm and exuberance over what God does with converted sinners. In 1 Peter 2:5, he calls the followers of Jesus living stones, a spiritual house, and a holy priesthood that offers spiritual sacrifices. In verse 9 they are called a chosen race, a royal priesthood, a holy nation, and God's own people. This assessment of the first-century church would, by virtue of the transmission of truth from generation to generation, be Peter's assessment of God's remnant people. For the remnant is the seed of the woman who represents God's people through the ages, and the remnant "keep the commandments of God, and have the testimony of Jesus Christ" (Revelation 12:17).

At first glance, some may think that verse 9 simply repeats the identifying characteristics Peter gives in verse 5. But careful examination reveals that two aspects of ancient Israel are represented—verse 5 presents the spiritual aspects and verse 9 the national. In verse 5 the followers of Jesus are said to be living stones built into a spiritual house where spiritual sacrifices are offered by a holy priesthood. In verse 9 they are referred to in terms of a race, a nation, a people, and they function as a royal priesthood. Thus they represent their Lord, who is King/Priest.

The spiritual aspects of God's people. The imagery of living stones being built into a spiritual house is an interesting one. The Greek language contains three words with various meanings for *stone* or *rock*. *Lithos* usually refers to a stone that has been worked by a craftsman, whether chiseled and shaped for use in construction or a precious stone used for ornamentation. *Petros* is a loose stone that lies upon the surface of the ground, while *petra* is a rock, or simply rock as opposed to some other material such as sand or metal. Peter uses the term *lithos*, thus indicating that each Christian is worked and shaped as he or she is prepared for a designated place in God's spiritual house.

Ellen White says:

> We are now in God's workshop. Many of us are rough stones from the quarry. But as the truth of God is brought to bear upon us, every imperfection is removed and we are prepared to shine as lively stones in the heavenly temple, where we shall be brought into association, not only with the holy angels, but with the King of heaven Himself.[1]

She gives two interpretations to the term *living stones*. First, she deals with the relationship between Jesus and the individual stones that are shaped and polished for use in the construction of God's spiritual house. As the foundation and cornerstone of His church, He is the great Living Stone. As each individual stone is added to the building, it draws life from the living Foundation, "Christ, the true foundation, is a living stone; His life is imparted to all that are built upon Him. . . . The stones became one with the foundation; for a common life dwells in all."[2]

She also speaks of these stones as being alive because the light and glory of heaven sparkles and dances as it reflects through them:

> How is Heaven amazed at the present condition of the church that could be so much to the world were every stone, in its proper place, a living stone to emit light. The stone that does not shine is worthless. That which constituted the value of our churches is not dead, lusterless stones; but living stones, stones that catch the bright beams from the chief corner stone, even from the Sun of Righteousness,—the bright glory in which are combined the beams of mercy and truth that have kissed each other.[3]

The spiritual house into which the followers of Jesus are built is the community of believers. This community practices no class, race, or sex discrimination (Galatians 3:28). All work together for the common good and toward a common goal—the advancement of the gospel.

Peter calls the followers of Jesus a holy priesthood who offer up spiritual sacrifices. In the previous chapter we saw how God gives the gift of holiness at the time of the new birth, and how, with the power of the Holy Spirit, the child of God becomes a victor over sin. On the basis of this experience, Peter can speak in terms of a holy priesthood. In verse 5, we are told that this priesthood offers spiritual sacrifices to God, which include thanksgiving and payment of vows (Psalm 50:14), a broken spirit and a broken and contrite heart (Psalm 51:17), and prayer (Psalm 141:2). Paul adds our bodies as a living sacrifice (Romans 12:1), love (Ephesians 5:1, 2), and faith (Philippians 2:17); the author of Hebrews suggests praise, good deeds, and sharing what we have (Hebrews 13:15, 16).

The national aspects of God's people. In 1 Peter 2:9, Peter talks in terms of national identity—"a chosen race, a royal priesthood, a holy nation, God's own people" (RSV). The terms used in both verses 5 and 9 were once applied to national Israel (Exodus 19:6; Deuteronomy 7:6). However, Peter clearly sees the position Israel once held as now being occupied by the followers of Jesus. The kingdom over which Jesus reigns comprises all people who respond to the gospel call.

As a race Israel was once chosen from among all the nations of the world to be God's people (Deuteronomy 7:6-11); now the followers of Jesus have become a chosen race in Him. But does God's selection of a new "chosen race" exclude members of the former? Paul says, No! "I say then, Hath God cast away his people? God forbid. For I also am an Israelite, of the seed of Abraham, of the tribe of Benjamin. God hath not cast away his people which he foreknew" (Romans 11:1, 2).

Because God calculates descent from Abraham on the basis of faith, not all who are physical descendants of Abraham are His children. "But it is not as though the word of God had failed. For not all who are descended from Israel belong to Israel, and not all are children of Abraham because they are his descendants; but 'Through Isaac shall your descendants be named' " (Romans 9:6, 7, RSV). Those among national Israel who believe in Christ, of whom Paul was a part, make up the true chosen people. "So too at the present time there is a remnant, chosen by grace.... Israel failed to obtain what it sought. The elect obtained it, but the rest were hardened" (Romans 11:5-7, RSV).

On the other hand, Peter says to his Gentile readers, "Once you were no people but now you are God's people; once you had not received mercy but now you have received mercy" (1 Peter 2:10, RSV). So all, both Jew and Gentile, who accept Christ as their personal Saviour become God's chosen race.

Paul explains how this is made possible: "Now to Abraham and his seed were the promises made. He saith not, And to seeds, as of many; but as of one, And to thy seed, which is Christ" (Galatians 3:16). Because all of the covenant promises were fulfilled in and received by Christ, God is shown to be the faithful, covenant-keeping God—His promises did not fail because Israel failed. Christ, who realized the fullness of all the covenant blessings, shares them with those who accept Him as their Saviour and Lord. So by faith in Christ, people of all nations become one (a chosen race)—children of Abraham (Galatians 3:7). Paul sums it all up this way: "If ye be Christ's, then are ye Abraham's seed, and heirs according to the promise" (Galatians 3:29).

As God's chosen race, His people not only become a holy nation but a royal priesthood to minister to the world.

Fruits of ministry. God intended that Israel should be a living demonstration to the surrounding nations of the mercy and blessings that were showered upon them.

> Had the Israelites obeyed the instruction they received, and profited by their advantages, they would have been the world's object lesson of health and prosperity. If as a people they had lived according to God's plan, they would have been preserved from the diseases that afflicted other nations. Above any other people they would have possessed physical strength and vigor of intellect.[4]

God intended that as the nations became acquainted with the laws by which Israel was to live, they would look upon Israel as a wise and understanding people, and praise the God who had given them their ordinances (Deuteronomy 4:5-8). Thus ancient Israel was to be a living witness to the glory of God. God's purpose for His chosen people remained the same in Peter's day and remains His purpose today: "That ye should shew forth the praises of him who hath called you out of darkness into his marvelous light" (1 Peter 2:9). The praises God's people render to God are manifested in obedience. This spirit of obedience identifies those who are truly God's people and those who make a hollow claim. Jesus discusses the fate of sham believers in Matthew 7:

> Not every one that saith unto me, Lord, Lord, shall enter into the kingdom of heaven; but he that doeth the will of my Father which is in heaven. Many will say to me in that day, Lord, Lord, have we not prophesied in thy name? and in thy name have cast out devils? and in thy name done many wonderful works? And then I will profess unto them, I never knew you: depart from me, ye that work iniquity (verses 21-23).

Summary

Christians today hold various ideas about the people of God, ranging from universalism, in which any and all are God's people, to denominational monopoly on God's favor. But the Bible clearly identifies them. They reveal their love for Jesus by their willing obedience, they possess the testimony that comes from Jesus, and they have the gift of faith. Peter presents them positively as living stones being built into a spiritual house. They are not only a holy priesthood that offers up spiritual sacrifices and ministers God's Word to a dying world, but as citizens in the kingdom of God, they are a chosen race, a royal priesthood, and a holy nation—God's own people.

---

1. *Child Guidance*, p. 73.
2. *Thoughts From the Mount of Blessing*, p. 150.
3. "Recount God's Dealings," *The Advent Review and Sabbath Herald*, March 19, 1895.
4. *Counsels on Diet and Foods*, p. 27.

Chapter 7
Civic Responsibilities

1 Peter 2:11-20

Every time the preacher began to talk about witnessing for Jesus, a strange phenomenon took place among his congregation. They became rigid in the pews as though they had been suddenly quick-frozen. Goose bumps appeared all over their flesh, the hair stood up on the back of their necks, their pupils dilated, and the palms of their hands began to sweat. The physical reaction to a simple word—*witnessing*—was absolutely amazing.

But Christians are born to witness, and Peter deals with this topic as he launches into a section on practical Christianity in his first epistle. In 1 Peter 2:11-20, he deals with the impact of a consistent Christian witness upon (1) the community in which the Christian lives, (2) government officials, and (3) households where Christian servants live. Within each of these contexts, he gives sound counsel to those who bear the name of Jesus.

Witness to the Community

Peter begins his instruction on effective community witnessing (verses 11, 12) by addressing his readers as "strangers and pilgrims." He first introduced the term *strangers* at 1:1, and the concept of a pilgrimage (*sojourn*, KJV) at 1:17. The term *pilgrim* suggests that Christians are not permanent residents in this world of sin. Their experience parallels that of Abraham, the father of the faithful, who was a pilgrim in a strange country while looking for the city that was to be his permanent home, "which hath foundations, whose builder and maker is God" (Hebrews 11:9, 10). The word *stranger* suggests that the things making this sinful world so attractive and exciting for some are foreign to those who count themselves as citizens of the New Jerusalem.

Peter bases the call to witness in the Christian warfare against the sinful attractions: "Dearly beloved, I beseech you as strangers and pilgrims, abstain from fleshly lusts, which war against the soul; having your conversation honest among the Gentiles [maintain good conduct among the Gentiles, RSV]" (verses 11, 12). Peter emphasizes two points: (1) turning away from fleshly lusts, and (2) dealing fairly and openly with the surrounding community.

Denial of fleshly lusts. In a previous chapter, we saw that all human beings have a fallen, sinful nature. This fallen nature is the seat of all passion and lust. Through the indwelling power of the Spirit of Christ, this nature can be brought under control. But only as we maintain a close relationship with Jesus will this be done. Paul says, "This I say then, Walk in the Spirit, and ye shall not fulfil the lust of the flesh. For the flesh lusteth against the Spirit, and the Spirit against the flesh: and these are contrary the one to the other: so that ye cannot do the things that ye would" (Galatians 5:16, 17).

The apostle assures us that if we choose to walk in the guidance of the Holy Spirit, He will continue to control the passions of our sinful natures and give us the victory over temptations that would overwhelm us if we battled them alone.

However, understanding the close relationship between the body, mind, and spirit, we can see that Peter's warning against indulging fleshly lusts has a broader meaning. Whatever gratifies bodily appetite and passion has a direct effect upon the mental and spiritual powers, and whatever affects the mind has an adverse impact upon the body and spirit. Therefore Ellen White says, "Whatever attracts the mind from God, whatever draws the affections away from Christ, is an enemy to the soul."[1]

Dealing fairly with the community. A Christian will not only be known for a life of strict morality, but also for his fairness and honesty in all his affairs. Where some will take advantage of others to advance their own interests, a true follower of Jesus will conduct his business, both personal and professional, with strict integrity. Where some will base their decisions on convenience, a Christian will stand on honesty and integrity.

> Strict honesty must be cultivated. We can go through the world but once; we cannot come back to rectify any mistakes; therefore every move made should be with godly fear and careful consideration. Honesty and policy [cunning stratagem] will not harmonize; either policy will be subdued, and truth and honesty hold the lines of control, or policy will take the lines, and honesty cease to direct. Both cannot act together; they can never be in agreement.[2]

Those who name the name of Jesus and then deal with their fellow citizens from a position of dishonest self-interest disgrace their Lord. Their condition is similar to the Jews in Rome: "Thou that makest thy boast of the law, through breaking the law dishonourest thou God? For the name of God is blasphemed among the Gentiles through you" (Romans 2:23, 24).

If Christians consistently practice purity and integrity, when the enemies of truth level accusations against God's remnant people, the community will see that the charges are false, and they will "see your good deeds and glorify God on the day of visitation" (1 Peter 2:12, RSV).

> Here, then, are two classes: one seeking for the pleas-

ures of this mortal life, the other for the enduring joys of immortality; one class are far from Christ, and satisfied with their condition, the other are seeking for the forgiveness of sins and for the Spirit of God; one class are battling against God and his truth, the other are warring against the lusts of the flesh, the spirit of the world, and Satan. One class are dreading the appearing of Christ, the Son of man, feeling that to them it is an overwhelming calamity; the other are looking for the coming of Christ the second time, without sin unto salvation. The one class will be rejected from the presence of God, and finally suffer the pangs of the second death; the other will have everlasting life at the right hand of God, where are pleasures for evermore.[3]

Witness to the Government

Peter carries his idea that a faithful Christian is a convincing witness for Jesus over to the arena of church/state relations. He says,

> Submit yourselves to every ordinance of man for the Lord's sake: whether it be to the king, as supreme; or unto governors, as unto them that are sent by him for the punishment of evildoers, and for the praise of them that do well. For so is the will of God, that with well doing ye may put to silence the ignorance of foolish men (1 Peter 2:13-15).

The Greek word that is translated "ordinance" (*ktisis*) in the KJV (verse 13) does not mean rules, regulations, or laws. *Ktisis* ("creation" or "creature") is the noun form of the verb *ktidzō*—"to people," "to found a city or colony" (in the Bible, "to create"). In 1 Peter, *ktisis* is better understood as "institution" (RSV), or something of human origin. In the case of governments, of course, while apparently founded by human beings, they are brought into existence with divine approval.

It is interesting that Peter tells his readers to be subject to governmental organizations "for the Lord's sake" (verse 13).

That is to say, for the sake of the Lord's cause in the earth. Is Peter possibly suggesting here that political activism by Christians can harm the cause of the gospel? In an age when evangelical Christians are becoming more politically active, many are asking, What should be the attitude of a Christian toward the government? Should Christians submit to those who rule and pray that their life's example will lead others to assume responsibility and become good leaders? Or should Christians actively seek to bring about political change?

The following statements illustrate the divergent opinions in Christian circles today:

1. "Christians should acknowledge the sovereignty of the divine providence in ordering and overruling human institutions and relations for men's good. The way, therefore, to please God, to serve His will, and to experience His blessing, is for Christians not to be rebels against the prevailing order of society, but rather positively, submissively and dutifully to discharge the various responsibilities which the common relations of life put upon them."[4]

2. "If the church wishes to exert an influence for good upon the State, it should not take recourse to separation but should try spiritual infiltration."[5]

Ellen White cautions against thoughtless words or actions that might provoke retaliation or persecution by the government, thus hindering Christian worship and outreach. On the other hand, she advises cooperation with civil authorities, as long as their requirements do not conflict with God's requirements:

> We are to recognize human government as an ordinance of divine appointment, and teach obedience to it as a sacred duty, within its legitimate sphere. But when its claims conflict with the claims of God, we must obey God rather than men. God's word must be recognized as above all human legislation. A "Thus saith the Lord" is not to be set aside for a "Thus saith the church" or a "Thus saith the state." The crown of Christ is to be lifted above the diadems of earthly potentates.[6]

While Christians submit themselves to governmental authority, they live as free people whose consciences are bound to no one but God (1 Peter 2:16). Those in bondage to other human beings have no physical freedom and must submit to another's will. Those in bondage to sin and passion may think they are free, but are truly slaves. Paradoxically, those in voluntary bondage to God have the highest degree of freedom and the peace that comes with the assurance of acceptance through their Saviour.

It is only the person in voluntary bondage to God who, (1) free from cultural and racial prejudice, can relate to all people as the product of His creation; (2) free from jealousy and the desire for supremacy, can love the community of believers unselfishly; (3) free from superstition and the bondage of satanic error, can give to God the reverence due Him; and (4) free from sloth and deceit, can render genuine service to his or her country.

God wills that ignorance and foolishness be countered by the blameless conduct of people who are truly free—people who freely choose to live respectable lives to the glory of God.

Witness of Christian Servants

In 2:18-20, Peter turns his attention to the third area in which Christians of his day had an opportunity to witness. He counsels servants to maintain an attitude of willful cooperation: "Servants, be subject to your masters with all fear; not only to the good and gentle, but also to the froward" (verse 18).

Peter recognized that not all masters were tyrants. He identifies some as being good and gentle. Being a household servant in such a situation would be relatively easy. The servant would find acceptance and security, and be supplied with food, clothing, and shelter. The close association with the family would present abundant opportunity for a Christian servant to bear a strong, positive witness for Jesus by his or her lifestyle and faithfulness to duty.

The Scriptures contain examples of servants who remained true to God and principle, allowing God to use them for the good of the home and the nation. Joseph in Potiphar's household (Genesis 39) and the Israelite maiden in Naaman's household (2 Kings 5) are outstanding examples.

The New Testament book of Philemon lets us look into a relationship between a Christian householder and a rebellious slave. In this reversed situation, Paul counsels the master to accept back into his home a servant who wronged him. Unfortunately, not all masters were of Philemon's caliber. Peter advises servants attached to tyrants to render faithful service, endure abuse, witness by spreading the love of Jesus throughout the household, and find satisfaction in God's approval.

In today's world we are more likely to experience employer/employee relationships than master/servant relationships, but the basic principles that Peter laid down would still apply. Strictest honesty must govern all dealings, and both parties should heed the following counsel:

> In every business transaction be rigidly honest. However tempted, never deceive or prevaricate in the least matter. At times a natural impulse may bring temptation to diverge from the straightforward path of honesty, but do not vary one hairsbreadth. . . . Carry out your agreement.[7]

> Belief in the near coming of the Son of man in the clouds of heaven will not cause the true Christian to become neglectful and careless of the ordinary business of life. The waiting ones who look for the soon appearing of Christ will not be idle, but diligent in business. Their work will not be done carelessly and dishonestly, but with fidelity, promptness, and thoroughness. Those who flatter themselves that careless inattention to the things of this life is an evidence of their spirituality and their separation from the world are under a great deception. Their veracity, faithfulness, and integrity are tested and proved in temporal things. If they are faithful in that which is least they will be faithful in much.[8]

However, where an employer is harsh and unjust, the employee might consider Peter's remaining counsel to servants—counsel that appeals to the great Servant Model, Jesus: "For this is trustworthy, if a man for conscience toward God endure grief, suffering wrongfully. For what glory is it, if, when ye be buffeted for your faults, ye shall take it patiently? but if, when ye do well, and suffer for it, ye take it patiently, this is acceptable with God" (verses 19, 20).

Suffering of various kinds will be inflicted upon the followers of Jesus, for the disciple is not greater than the Master. However, suffering, no matter how it is inflicted, need not separate us from our Lord:

> We should not allow our feelings to be easily wounded. We are to live, not to guard our feelings or our reputation, but to save souls. As we become interested in the salvation of souls we cease to mind the little differences that so often arise in our association with one another. Whatever others may think of us or do to us, it need not disturb our oneness with Christ, the fellowship of the Spirit.[9]

Summary

As Peter begins the pastoral section of his first epistle, he appeals to his readers to bear a positive witness for Jesus and their faith (1) in the community, (2) before rulers, and (3) in their daily work; "for this is acceptable to God."

---

1. *Christ's Object Lessons*, p. 53.
2. *Seventh-day Adventist Bible Commentary*, vol. 6, p. 1081.
3. "The Coming of the Lord," *Signs of the Times*, Nov. 10, 1887.
4. Alan M. Stibbs, "The First Epistle General of Peter," *Tyndale New Testament Commentaries* (Grand Rapids: Wm. B. Eerdmans Publishing Company, 1971) p. 106.
5. William Hendriksen, "Romans," cited by Simon J. Kistemaker, "Exposi-

tion of the Epistles of Peter and of the Epistle of Jude," *New Testament Commentary* (Grand Rapids: Baker Book House, 1987), p. 103.
  6. *The Acts of the Apostles*, p. 69.
  7. *Child Guidance*, p. 154.
  8. *Testimonies for the Church*, vol. 4, p. 309.
  9. *The Ministry of Healing*, p. 485.

Chapter 8
Walking in His Footsteps

1 Peter 2:20-25

For those of you who have never done it, let me assure you that walking through deep snow is no easy task. When the snow is up to your waist, putting one foot in front of the other is strenuous work; and if a person has to walk any distance, he or she is soon exhausted. A walk that would be nearly impossible for a child becomes almost easy if he or she can walk in an adult's footsteps.

In 1 Peter 2:20-25, the apostle discusses suffering. This passage continues the counsel that Peter gives to Christian servants who suffer at the hands of overbearing masters (2:18-20). If all Christians, not only servants, who find themselves in difficult circumstances would lift up their eyes, they would see that Someone is walking ahead of them, making the path of suffering easier than if they had to struggle on alone.

Peter holds up Jesus as the Model Sufferer. If we keep our eyes on Him and understand His suffering, it will help us deal with our pain, frustration, and disappointment in two ways: (1) we will eventually realize that He suffered more intensely than we ever will, and (2) we will see how suffering can be endured to the glory of God. Simon Kistemaker says, "We follow Christ not in the degree of anguish and pain but in the manner in which he endured suffering."[1]

As Peter addresses those servants who were being treated unjustly, he sets forth two results of Jesus' suffering: (1) He is an example to be followed—the Model Sufferer, and (2) by His suffering He has become the substitute, the ransom for the human race. Both of these points deserve study.

The Perfect Example

As Peter wrote verses 21-23, the scenes in Caiaphas's house probably came rushing back to his mind. He had witnessed enough of Jesus' suffering to speak with authority on the subject. He saw Jesus mocked, ridiculed, spit upon, and physically abused—without striking back. So Peter says to all who are abused, "If, when ye do well, and suffer for it, ye take it patiently, this is acceptable with God. For even hereunto were ye called: because Christ also suffered for us, leaving us an example, that ye should follow his steps" (1 Peter 2:20, 21).

What makes Jesus' patient endurance under abuse so amazing is that He possessed the power and authority to destroy His persecutors.

> Christ suffered keenly under abuse and insult. At the hands of the beings whom He had created, and for whom He was making an infinite sacrifice, He received every indignity. And He suffered in proportion to the perfection of His holiness and His hatred of sin. His trial by men who acted as fiends was to Him a perpetual sacrifice. To be surrounded by human beings under the control of Satan was revolting to Him. And He knew that in a moment, by the flashing forth of His divine power, He could lay His cruel tormentors in the dust. This made the trial the harder to bear.[2]

Peter continues the report of what he witnessed at Jesus' trial: "Who did no sin, neither was guile found in his mouth: Who, when he was reviled, reviled not again; when he suffered, he threatened not; but committed himself to him that judgeth righteously" (verses 22, 23). While suffering more abuse than we are called upon to bear, Jesus did not sin by thinking a wrong thought, speaking a wrong word, or engaging in a wrong act.

As we undergo abuse and injustice, or as we relive in our memories abuse we have received, how often we fantasize. We imagine that we possess power to bring the persecutors to their knees, to force them to respect us and to treat us fairly. Jesus possessed that power. He could have reduced the entire assembly gathered for His trial to sniveling suppliants, pleading for His mercy; more than that, He could have terminated them with a word. But He did not retaliate. He submitted. The Creator, the great God, the Monarch of the universe submitted to the cruelest indignities that His demon-possessed creatures could heap upon Him.

> His love for His Father, and His pledge, made from the foundation of the world, to become the Sin Bearer, led Him to endure uncomplainingly the coarse treatment of those He came to save. It was a part of His mission to bear, in His humanity, all the taunts and abuse that men could heap upon Him. The only hope of humanity was in this submission of Christ to all that He could endure from the hands and hearts of men.[3]

Having witnessed it all, Peter says, "Follow his steps" (verse 21). Can it be done? Can a human being endure as Jesus endured and honor Him by patiently suffering for His name and His cause? Yes, it can and has been done. "As they were stoning Stephen, he prayed, 'Lord Jesus, receive my spirit.' And he knelt down and cried with a loud voice, 'Lord, do not hold this sin against them.' And when he had said this, he fell asleep" (Acts 7:59, 60, RSV). Stephen is only the first of millions down through the centuries who endured suffering for Jesus. Yes, it can be done, but only as a human being is possessed by the same Spirit that filled Jesus.

At this point in the history of God's end-time people, not too many of us have been called upon to make the sacrifice that Stephen made for the cause of Jesus. The abuse and indignity that we suffer is small compared to what he and Jesus went through. We must be careful not to let the enemy of our souls get a foothold through little annoyances he brings upon us.

Jesus is our example in patient endurance and control of thought, word, and deed. In nothing did He sin.

Sin Bearer

The second result of Jesus' suffering is our redemption. "Who his own self bare our sins in his own body on the tree, that we, being dead to sins, should live unto righteousness: by whose stripes ye were healed" (verse 24). This verse contains two key thoughts: (1) Jesus is our substitute, and (2) through His suffering we are free to live a life of righteousness.

Jesus our substitute. The entire plan of saving humanity from the penalty of sin is rooted in substitution. The ancient sanctuary service clearly teaches this. The sacrifices brought to the altar, the blood of the victim sprinkled and poured out were all a substitute pointing toward the Divine Substitute for the guilty person who should have died. Jesus bore our sins to the cross so we will not have to bear them. He is our Substitute.

This concept is readily accepted in the Christian world, but an accompanying idea presented in Scripture—the idea of ransom—makes many uncomfortable. The discomfort may result from the legal implications of a ransom's being paid—implications leading to questions such as, What demand does Jesus satisfy as a ransom, and to whom is the ransom paid?

The word *ransom* (*lutron*, Matthew 20:28; Mark 10:45; or *antilutron*, 1 Timothy 2:6) comes from the verb *lutroō* which is translated "redeemed" (Luke 24:21; Titus 2:14; 1 Peter 1:18). Thus the word *to redeem* has the idea of ransom within it. I suppose the concept of ransom is not that far removed from substitute. When a ransom is paid, the ransom becomes a substitute for the person or item that is held.

Theologians have debated to whom the ransom is paid. Two suggestions have been offered—God and Satan. But because both possibilities are illogical, many dismiss the idea of Jesus being a ransom. However, Jesus Himself said that He had come to give His life as a ransom (*lutron*) for many (Matthew 20:28; Mark 10:45). One explanation is that although material ransoms are paid to individuals, the receiver of a spiritual ransom does not have to be specified. However, if *ransom* can be thought of as a synonym for *substitute*, the problem might be resolved.

Yet the idea of being freed from something lingers in the word *ransom*. This is seen in the verb *redeemed* (*lutroō*), which is the root for *ransom* (*lutron*). For example, the disciples walking to Emmaus said to Jesus, "We trusted that it had been he which should have redeemed [*lutroō*, ransomed] Israel" (Luke 24:21). The same nuance can be found in Paul, "Who gave himself for us, that he might redeem [*lutroō*, ransom] us from all iniquity" (Titus 2:14); and in Peter, "Ye know that ye were not redeemed [*lutroō*, ransomed] with corruptible things, as silver and gold, from your vain conversation" (1 Peter 1:18).

It is possible that the word *ransom* in the New Testament bears the ideas of substitution and freedom without specifying a payment being made to someone.

But, once again, one returns to the legal aspect of Jesus' death. Death is present in our world because of sin (Romans 5:12, 13). Our first parents rebelled against God and violated His word and His law, causing death to pass upon us all. Because of Adam's rebellion, we all possess a fallen nature, a propensity to sin, and are under the sentence of death. Jesus' substitutionary death (ransom) satisfied the legal demands of death for violators. Thus the sinner is redeemed (ransomed), and the law remains intact. This line of reasoning suggests that a ransom, alone, is inadequate. The law remains in force: people are still bound to obey it.

Free to live a life of righteousness. By bearing to the cross our sins in His body, Jesus provides the means for us to leave behind sinful practices. Repeatedly Peter impresses upon the minds of his readers in various ways that the followers of Jesus are not to tolerate sin in their lives. We have seen several examples of this in previous chapters. Peter returns to this theme again in verse 24: "We, being dead to sins, should live unto righteousness."

The Greek word translated "dead" (KJV) or "die" (RSV) has a primary meaning of "to be removed from," or "depart." The idea of dying is a derivative meaning. If we understand this verse in the light of the primary meaning, we can again see Peter calling Christians to a victorious life by abandoning sin through the power so generously given by Jesus. But this is not all; Peter says that in Jesus the believer is free to live "unto righteousness." That is, to live in a righteous way or to follow a righteous lifestyle.

We have dealt with this concept in some detail in a previous chapter. The fact that Peter comes back to the truth that a Christian is to live a life free from sinful acts only emphasizes the importance of this experience in Christ. We do not preach enough on this point. We fail to teach it and indoctrinate new members with this idea. Let me emphasize again what was stressed in the former chapter. When we talk in terms of living a life of victory over sin, we are not speaking in terms of a triumphal display of our righteousness before the congregation of our church. We are speaking, rather, in terms of victory over sin through the indwelling power of the Spirit of Christ. We are speaking of an attitude that emerges from the stark realization that we are sinful by nature and that we have no hope or help outside of Jesus.

When we are living unto righteousness, we will reflect in our lives the fruits of righteousness. We will deny ungodliness and worldly lusts, and live soberly and righteously in this present world as Paul admonished Titus (2:11, 12). Ellen White reflects the optimism found in Peter's writings. She assures us that, under the guidance of the Holy Spirit, the fallen, sinful nature will not dominate us when we surrender to Jesus, and that victory over sinful acts can be ours.

Speaking of the joy Jesus shares in the victories of His followers, Ellen White wrote:

> Christ rejoiced that He could do more for His followers

than they could ask or think. He spoke with assurance, knowing that an almighty decree had been given before the world was made. He knew that truth, armed with the omnipotence of the Holy Spirit, would conquer in the contest with evil; and that the bloodstained banner would wave triumphantly over His followers. He knew that the life of His trusting disciples would be like His, a series of uninterrupted victories, not seen to be such here, but recognized as such in the great hereafter.[4]

Finally, Peter assures us that we have been healed by the wounds that Jesus suffered and that the great Shepherd and Guardian of the flock will keep and preserve us. Again he returns to a concept presented earlier in his epistle. Those who have accepted Him are precious in His sight, and He will not allow the enemy to snatch them from His protecting hand. We can rest in the assurance of victory and protection. This truth must be impressed upon the minds of His people. This assurance must burn within their hearts.

Summary

Jesus' patient endurance under abuse and indignity is the example that all of His followers are called to follow. But He is more than a moral example for His people; He is their substitute, their ransom. He purchased them through His blood, and by the power of His indwelling spirit, they have died to sin and live a life of holiness. There is victory in His blood.

---

1. Simon J. Kistemaker, *Exposition of the Epistles of Peter and of the Epistle of Jude* (Grand Rapids: Baker Book House, 1987), p. 109.

2. *The Desire of Ages*, p. 700.

3. Ibid., p. 703.

4. Ibid., p. 679.

Chapter 9
To Love, Honor, and Cherish

1 Peter 3:1-7

Every time I pick up *The Desire of Ages* and read the first three pages, I pause in awe, trying to absorb the concepts presented there. They contain a new approach to an understanding of God's law—the foundation for governing heaven and the earth. They present true love, as well as reveal selfishness in all of its ugliness.

These pages point out that self-renouncing love is the sum and substance of God's law. It is "the great principle which is the law of life for the universe." It can be seen "shining in the face of Jesus" and "in the light from Calvary."[1] As Christ brought this world into existence, He wrote the message of the Father's love upon all creation. Though marred by sin, nature still proclaims God's law. All created things—the birds, the animals, the trees, the grass, the sun, the moon, the clouds, the rivers, the oceans—give of themselves to minister to others. Even heavenly angels rejoice when giving of themselves in service and tireless watch care over fallen humanity. "There is nothing, save the selfish heart of man, that lives unto itself."[2]

In Christ we see the greatest revelation of God's law.

> All things Christ received from God, but He took to give. So in the heavenly courts, in His ministry for all created beings: through the beloved Son, the Father's life flows out to all; through the Son it returns, in praise and joyous service, a tide of love, to the great Source of all. And thus through Christ the circuit of beneficence is complete, representing the character of the great Giver, the law of life.
>
> In heaven itself this law was broken. Sin originated in self-seeking. Lucifer, the covering cherub, desired to be first in heaven.[3]

The root of sin lies in selfishness. For this reason Lucifer is unable to understand why Jesus would become a man and die for the human race:

> At the birth of Jesus, Satan knew that One had come with a divine commission to dispute his dominion. He trembled at the angel's message attesting the authority of the newborn King. Satan well knew the position that Christ had held in heaven as the Beloved of the Father. That the Son of God should come to this earth as a man filled him with amazement and with apprehension. He could not fathom the mystery of this great sacrifice. His selfish soul could not understand such love for the deceived race.[4]

Lucifer had charged God with injustice when he was banished from heaven, saying that even God Himself could not live by His own law. But Jesus' incarnation and death on the cross show the lie in Lucifer's statement. As we look to Jesus and the cross, we see God abiding by the demands of His own law—self-renouncing love. In the incarnation and at Calvary, the universe had a revelation of God that had never before been seen, even throughout the ages of eternity past. The inhabitants of the universe had never before seen God challenged. While watching Lucifer reveal the nature of sin, they also watched a new light being shed upon the nature of God.

> By coming to dwell with us, Jesus was to reveal God both to men and to angels. . . . Our little world is the lesson book of the universe. God's wonderful purpose of grace, the mystery of redeeming love, is the theme into which "angels desire to look," and it will be their study throughout endless ages. Both the redeemed and the unfallen beings will find in the cross of Christ their science and their song. It will be seen that the glory shining in the face of Jesus is the glory of self-sacrificing love.[5]

Peter is aware that the great drama of the universe is played out in the home of every follower of Jesus. In every family, the powers of self-renouncing love and selfishness struggle for dominance. Where the principle of self-renouncing love is encouraged and nurtured, the home is a foretaste of heaven. Where selfishness dominates, the home is a living hell. As we progress in this chapter, we will see that Peter's counsel (1 Peter 3:1-7) is based upon the principle of self-renouncing love, the basis of the law of life for earth and heaven.

Counsels for Wives

Of the seven verses dealing with family relations, Peter devotes six to counsel for Christian wives and one to Christian husbands. The verses addressed to wives deal with three topics: (1) the wife's relationship with her husband, (2) her relationship with God, and (3) the example set by holy women in the Old Testament.

Wife/husband relationship. Peter begins his counsel on family relations with the word *likewise.* This word ties Peter's counsel to what immediately precedes it—Christian lifestyle (2:11, 12), responsibilities of citizenship (2:13-17), and relationships between slaves and masters (2:18-25). The instruction to wives (3:1-6) and husbands (3:7—notice the repetition of *likewise* in verse 7) is a part of Peter's broader view of how God's law of self-renouncing love enters into all interpersonal relationships.

Peter's instruction that wives are to be submissive to their husbands (verse 3) is in agreement with the counsel given by Paul to his readers (Ephesians 5:22; Colossians 3:18; 1 Timothy 2:11, 12). But this is not to be a blind submission. Paul recognizes that husband and wife stand on equal footing before Jesus: "There is neither male nor female: for ye are all one in Christ Jesus" (Galatians 3:28). Peter, similarly, hastens to remind the husband that he and his wife are joint heirs in God's plan of salvation (1 Peter 3:7). Ellen White says, "Woman should fill the position which God originally designed for her, as her husband's equal."[6] The wife's submission is simply a recognition that the husband and father merely serves as team leader in the family circle composed of members equal in God's eyes.

The Christian family will be structured on the basis of God's law of self-renouncing love. Although designated team leader, the husband will seek the interests and well-being of the wife and children above his own personal interests. The reverse is also true: the wife and children will each seek first the interests and well-being of the team leader and others on the team. If this principle is maintained, selfishness will not be allowed to spoil the happiness of all.

As is true today, when Peter wrote his epistle, not all church members represented families united in Christ. As the gospel spread throughout the Roman Empire, many homes became divided in their religious affiliation. The problems that arose were, perhaps, not much different from those faced in divided homes today. While the early church faced the difficulties of the gospel entering Jewish and pagan homes and dividing the religious interests, the entrance of the three angels' messages into a Christian home today can cause similar problems. If one of the marriage partners accepts present truth, how is that person to relate to the one who does not?

Peter suggests that if the believing spouse will live by the principle of self-renouncing love, the unbelieving spouse will see the beauty of Christ's character reflected in the life and may be won to the religious beliefs of the spouse (verses 1, 2). Provided, of course, the believing spouse does not compromise his or her belief in an endeavor to demonstrate self-renouncing love.

Paul, however, evidently knew of instances in which an unbelieving spouse refused to remain with the believing spouse once the gospel entered the home. His counsel in such a situation: "If the unbelieving depart, let him depart. A brother or a sister is not under bondage in such cases: but God hath called us to peace" (1 Corinthians 7:15). However, if the unbelieving spouse departs, this constitutes only a separation, and the believing spouse is not free to remarry unless biblical grounds exist.

Wife/God relationship. In dealing with the relationship between the wife and her God, Peter again stresses the principle that lies at the very foundation of God's eternal law. God wants those who represent Him in the world to be adorned with "the hidden man of the heart, in that which is not corruptible, even the ornament of a meek and quiet spirit, which is in the sight of God of great price" (verse 4). Peter is clear that God does not want the women in His church to follow the customs of the world, adorning themselves as the women in the world do.

Paul gives similar counsel, "In like manner also, that women adorn themselves in modest apparel, with shamefacedness and sobriety; not with broided hair, or gold, or pearls, or costly array; but (which becometh women professing godliness) with good works" (1 Timothy 2:9, 10). As the Christian relates to her God on the basis of self-renouncing love, she will lay aside those things that displease God and will seek His interests first.

The basic principles laid down by Peter and Paul relating to physical adornment apply to men as well as to women. The men in the church cannot consider themselves free from the admonitions relating to physical appearance. They too are representatives of Jesus and must build their relationship with God upon the principle of self-renouncing love.

> The apostle presents the inward adorning, in contrast with the outward, and tells us what the great God values. The outward is corruptible. But the meek and quiet spirit, the development of a beautifully symmetrical

character, will never decay. It is an adornment which is not perishable. In the sight of the Creator of everything that is valuable, lovely, and beautiful it is declared to be of great price.[7]

There are many whose hearts have been so hardened by prosperity that they forget God, and forget the wants of their fellow men. Professed Christians adorn themselves with jewelry, laces, costly apparel, while the Lord's poor suffer for the necessaries of life. Men and women who claim redemption through a Saviour's blood will squander the means intrusted to them for the saving of other souls, and then grudgingly dole out their offerings for religion, giving liberally only when it will bring honor to themselves. These are idolaters.[8]

Holy women in the Old Testament. In appealing to the example of women in the Old Testament, Peter holds up a standard for his readers. These women were in subjection to their husbands as team leaders, and they adorned themselves according to the law of self-renouncing love (verses 5, 6). There is, however, an added thought by Peter on "adorning" in verse 5. The word *subjection* (KJV) or *submissive* (RSV) is a participle that explains what Peter meant by using the verb *adorn.* The adornment that Peter emphasizes here is the spirit of submission. The verse might read something like this, "For after this manner in the old time the holy women also, who trusted in God, adorned themselves with submission to their own husbands."

Sarah is held up as the supreme example to the women in the church. Even the holy women of old who came after Sarah are compared to her, "being in subjection unto their own husbands: even as Sara obeyed Abraham, calling him lord." Peter's source for saying that Sarah called Abraham lord is not quite clear. It may have been a bit of tradition that had been passed on from generation to generation. However, Peter's statement does not exaggerate the respect that Sarah had for her husband.

As Abraham is recognized by Paul as the father of those who have faith in God (Galatians 3:29), so Sarah is recognized by Peter as the mother of Christian women who are rich in good works and who have courageous hearts.

Peter tells us that these women trusted (hoped) in God. Some commentators believe that their trust or hope in God involved not only their eternal salvation, but also the hope that they would be the mother of the promised Messiah. If this is true, we might also list the great matriarchs who were the Messiah's forerunners. The list includes not only Sarah, but Rebecca (wife of Isaac and mother of Jacob), Leah (wife of Jacob and mother of Judah), Tamar (who bore Perez and Zerah, illegitimate twins, for Judah, Matthew 1:3), Rahab the harlot (Matthew 1:5), Ruth the Moabitess (Matthew 1:5), and Bathsheba (wife of Uriah, mistress of David, and mother of Solomon, Matthew 1:6). All were forerunners of the Messiah, and all depended on Him for forgiveness.

Counsels for Husbands

Peter bases his counsel for Christian husbands upon the same principle that underlies the counsel given to wives—self-renouncing love. In fact, it seems that if each husband followed Peter's advice, the church would be filled with happy women.

Peter lays the burden upon the husband to become knowledgeable with respect to his wife. As he comes to know her, he will give her due respect and honor. Following the example set by the team leader, the children will, in turn, hold her in respect, and all will look upon each other as joint heirs of the grace of their Lord.

Following the positive advice on husband-and-wife relationships, it is interesting that Peter closes this section with a thinly veiled threat to husbands. If the husband fails to treat his wife with respect and honor as a joint heir of salvation, his prayers will go unheard (verse 7)—a threat that should lead any Christian husband to evaluate his relationship with his wife.

Summary

We can now put the whole picture together. God's eternal law by which He governs the vast universe is stated in one simple principle—self-renouncing love. Those who abide by this law will place the interest of others before their own, as long as the interests of others do not conflict with the principle of self-renouncing love.

As this is applied to the family, the husband will seek to fulfill the interests of his wife, and she will seek to fulfill the interests of her husband. Together they will seek to fulfill the interest and desire of their God. For this reason, the family will treasure the instruction given in His Word and will base their choices of lifestyle and activities on its principles.

The principle extends beyond the family. As we relate to God on the basis of self-renouncing love, so He deals with us on the basis of the same principle. The cross provides the greatest demonstration of self-renouncing love. It is God's answer to Satan's accusations that He cannot obey His own law.

So the members of the Christian family seek to fill the interests of God in a relationship of self-renouncing love, and God seeks the interests of the family as He gives of Himself for their earthly happiness and eternal joy.

---

1. *The Desire of Ages*, pp. 21, 20.
2. Ibid., p. 20.
3. Ibid., p. 21.
4. Ibid., p. 115.
5. Ibid., pp. 19, 20.
6. *The Adventist Home*, p. 231.
7. *My Life Today*, p. 123.
8. *Seventh-day Adventist Bible Commentary*, vol. 2, p. 1012.

Chapter 10
Defend the Faith

1 Peter 3:8-22

Peter commented that the writings of the apostle Paul contain some things that are hard to understand (2 Peter 3:15, 16). I am not sure, however, that much in Paul's epistles will rival in difficulty Peter's statement about the spirits in prison. These are the puzzling verses:

> For Christ also hath once suffered for sins, the just for the unjust, that he might bring us to God, being put to death in the flesh, but quickened by the Spirit: By which also he went and preached unto the spirits in prison; which sometime were disobedient, when once the longsuffering of God waited in the days of Noah, while the ark was a preparing, wherein few, that is, eight souls were saved by water (1 Peter 3:18-20).

Commentators on biblical passages generally root their interpretations in doctrinal positions—in this case, the doctrine of the state of the dead. If a person believes that the Bible teaches spirit consciousness after death, then the idea of

Jesus' preaching between His crucifixion and resurrection to the spirits of those who rejected Noah's message is perfectly logical. Charles Biggs's commentary on 1 Peter serves as an illustration of this popular interpretation:

> After our Lord's Death He still lived and ministered. . . . There can be no doubt that the event referred to is placed between the Crucifixion and the Ascension.
> What St. Peter says is that Christ not only ministered to men upon earth, but also . . . went as a spirit to preach to spirits in prison. Of these spirits we are told that they had been disobedient in the days of Noah.[1]

If, however, one believes that the Bible teaches death to be sleep, then we must let that biblical doctrine determine the meaning of Peter's words. Doctrine, then, no matter how dry and boring to some people, becomes crucial for properly understanding a difficult passage.

Importance of Doctrine

The following warning by Ellen White points out the importance of sound doctrinal beliefs:

> Rebellion and apostasy are in the very air we breathe. We shall be affected by it unless we by faith hang our helpless souls upon Christ. If men are so easily misled, how will they stand when Satan shall personate Christ, and work miracles? Who will be unmoved by his misrepresentations, professing to be Christ when it is only Satan assuming the person of Christ, and apparently working the works of Christ? What will hold God's people from giving their allegiance to false christs? "Go ye not . . . after them" (Luke 21:8).
> The doctrines must be plainly understood. The men accepted to teach the truth must be anchored; then their vessel will hold against storm and tempest, because the anchor holds them firmly. The deceptions will increase.[2]

DEFEND THE FAITH 91

The following well-known prediction again emphasizes the importance of correct doctrinal positions: "Through the two great errors, the immortality of the soul and Sunday sacredness, Satan will bring the people under his deceptions."[3]

A correct doctrinal understanding of the state of the dead and the Sabbath of God will prove to be a part of the protecting hedge around God's people while the rest of Christendom is swept away by Satan's final delusions. As Satan quoted Scripture to Jesus as part of the wilderness temptations, so he uses Scripture to draw Christians who have been taught spurious doctrines into his final deceptions.

Let me illustrate this point. A well-known writer on religious cults spoke to a group of people about Seventh-day Adventist beliefs. Having stated several times that he was a friend of Seventh-day Adventists, he proceeded to hold up a number of our doctrines to scorn and ridicule. One that he touched upon briefly was our understanding of the biblical teaching on the state of the dead.

He based his criticism on Paul's statement that he was torn between departing so he could be with the Lord and continuing in the flesh so he could minister to the needs of the followers of Christ (Philippians 1:21-23). The speaker said:

> Adventists believe that when you die, you go into a state of unconsciousness, waiting for the resurrection. The Apostle Paul doesn't agree with them. In Philippians, chapter 1, he says, "I long to depart and be with Christ; which is far better." The word "depart" means "weigh anchor." Paul says, "I long to weigh anchor and be with Jesus." What happens to your boat when you weigh anchor? Does it stay where it is? No, it drifts or it goes under other power. Paul says, "I long to depart and be with Christ: that's far better."
>
> I was talking to an Adventist theologian about this a while back. He said, "What you don't understand is that the Apostle Paul is saying here that when Jesus comes back again, then we're going to be with Him." I said,

That's a marvelous interpretation. There's only one problem with it. The next verse says, "Or to stay here, which is more necessary for you." If Paul's talking about the second coming of Jesus Christ, he won't have to stay there for them because they're going too.[4]

Now, how would you answer the challenge that the speaker levels against our understanding of the state of the dead? Because Philippians 1:23 has been used repeatedly against our teaching of conditional immortality, and because the subject of this verse relates to the issue raised in 1 Peter 3:19, 20, perhaps we should answer the speaker's challenge before we return to Peter's spirits in prison. In the process, we might demonstrate the importance of doctrine and the weakness in the arguments against conditional immortality.

New Testament Teaching on Death

Those who assume that the Bible teaches a conscious state in death use Philippians 1:23 as evidence that the Christian enters into the presence of the Lord at the moment of death. However, the New Testament uses the metaphor of sleep to teach what happens at the moment of death. For example, the most frequently used word for this metaphor is *koimaomai* (passive form of *koimaō*), appearing eighteen times (Matthew 27:52; 28:13; Luke 22:45; John 11:11, 12; Acts 7:60; 12:6; 13:36; 1 Corinthians 7:39; 11:30; 15:6, 18, 20, 51; 1 Thessalonians 4:13, 14, 15; 2 Peter 3:4). Of these eighteen appearances, only three refer to natural sleep (Matthew 28:13; Luke 22:45; Acts 12:6); the remaining fifteen speak of death as a sleep. Four additional words in the New Testament are used for sleep, but only *katheudō* (three out of twenty-two appearances, Matthew 9:24; Mark 5:39; Luke 8:52—all referring to Jairus's daughter) is used for death.

A bit of quiet omission is needed if someone uses Philippians 1:23 to attack our position on the state of the dead. People are not told that of the fifteen appearances of *koimaomai* (sleep) as a metaphor for death, nine are in the writings of Paul (see 1 Corinthians 7:39; 11:30; 15:6, 18, 20,

51; 1 Thessalonians 4:13-15). In an attempt to understand what Paul meant when he said that he desired to depart and to be with Jesus, do we ignore these nine verses that clearly show Paul's understanding of death as a sleep? That is to say, Do we interpret nine verses on the basis of what one says, or do we interpret one on the basis of the nine? To brush away the nine would be dishonest with what Paul is teaching about death. Proper interpretation would demand that what Paul says about departing and being with the Lord in Philippians 1:23 must be understood in light of the nine references in his epistles to death as a sleep.

If death is an unconscious state (sleep), what does Paul mean when he says he desires to depart and be with the Lord? To understand his statement, we must do a word study. The Greek word translated "to depart" appears only twice in the New Testament in its verb form (*analuō*, Luke 12:36 [where it means "to return"], and Philippians 1:23), and only once in its noun form (*analusis*, 2 Timothy 4:6). Other words for *depart* are preferred in the New Testament. *Analuō* literally means "to loose or undo again." It is used in classical Greek for hoisting an anchor (navy) and for breaking camp (army). It describes what is done in preparation for departure and not the act of departing itself. Paul, however, uses it as a euphemism for death. Even today, we employ the same euphemism in an attempt to conceal the fear and terror that we feel when we talk about death. For example, when we tell someone that Aunt Nellie has "departed," it is a comfortable way of saying she is dead.

Because Paul contributes nine verses to the New Testament doctrine of conditional immortality, how, then, are we to understand Philippians 1:23? What is missing in this verse is a reference to the lapse of time between the act of breaking camp and seeing the Lord. For, according to Paul, a period of sleep separates the two experiences. However, Paul assumes that his readers would know this on the basis of the teaching by the New Testament church that death is an unconscious state. Events separated by time are often spoken of in Scripture in such a way that the reader would assume a close proximity between the events, only to learn of the time element as a result of further reading.

For example, if we had only Luke's Gospel, we would assume on the basis of chapter 24 that Jesus ascended to His Father on the same day He was raised from the dead. However, Acts 1:3 tells us His ascension was forty days after the resurrection. Luke 24 does not inform us of the time that separated the resurrection and the ascension. Also, Jesus told the Sanhedrin that the time would come when the dead would hear the voice of the Son of God. Those who have done good will be raised to life and those who have done evil to damnation (John 5:29). Jesus did not bring out the fact at that time that there would be 1,000 years between the two resurrections. We find that out in Revelation 20.

To build a doctrinal teaching on one text while ignoring nine others that contradict the resulting theological position is sloppy exegesis.

The Spirits in Prison

Now we return to the passage discussing spirits who are in prison. It is clear that New Testament writers used the metaphor of sleep to describe the experience of death. This, then, can be said to be the New Testament doctrine on the state of the dead. How can this doctrinal teaching help us understand what Peter says about the spirits in prison?

First of all, when Jesus died upon the cross, He entered into a state that the New Testament describes as sleep. Therefore, between the crucifixion and the resurrection, He was in a condition of unconsciousness. Second, if the spirits to whom He preached were alive on earth during the time of Noah, as the passage says, they would also have been dead—asleep or unconscious—at the time of Jesus' ministry on earth. As a result, it would have been impossible for Jesus to preach to them at that time.

The New Testament doctrine on the state of the dead makes the popular interpretation of this passage unacceptable. The only understanding that this doctrine will permit is that, by some means, the people of Noah's day were addressed by Jesus prior to their deaths. Can this be seen in the passage? Yes, it can.

First Peter 3:18 concludes with the statement that Jesus was brought back from the state of death *by* the power of the Spirit. Verse 19 begins with a prepositional phrase, *by which*. The antecedent of *which* is the Spirit at the end of verse 18 who brought Jesus back from death. In both instances the idea of agency is being communicated. So the Holy Spirit was the Agent by whom Jesus was quickened or made alive, and the Agent by whom Jesus preached the call to repentance and the warning of coming destruction to those who were imprisoned. Noah and his helpers were, in turn, the agents used by the Holy Spirit. And how were these people in Noah's day imprisoned? They were imprisoned by sin and unbelief, not by physical death—at least not during the warning.

The keys that unlock the meaning of this passage are: (1) understanding that the words *by the Spirit* at the end of verse 18 and that the prepositional phrase (*by which*) at the beginning of verse 19 indicate agency and (2) understanding the New Testament doctrine of the state of the dead.

The RSV, however, reveals the presupposition that there is consciousness after death when it renders verses 18 and 19, "Being put to death in the flesh but made alive in the spirit; in which he went and preached to the spirits in prison." This rendering of the passage suggests that Jesus, in a disembodied form, after His death, and before His resurrection, preached in the spirit world to the spirits of those who rejected the appeals of Noah and were in the prison house of death. The KJV is true to the teaching of the New Testament on the state of death when it says that Jesus was "quickened *by* the Spirit" (agency) and that it was *by* this Spirit (agency) that He preached to "the spirits in prison [sin and unbelief] . . . when once the longsuffering of God waited in the days of Noah, while the ark was a preparing."

Ellen White takes her position with the New Testament writers when she says, "During this time, while the ark was building, the voices of Noah, Methuselah, and many others were heard in warning and entreaty, and every blow struck on the ark was a warning message."[5] " 'For this purpose the Son of God was manifested, that He might destroy the works of the devil.' Christ was engaged in this warfare in Noah's day. It was His voice that spoke to the inhabitants of the old world in messages of warning, reproof, and invitation."[6]

Defend the Faith

Now that we see the importance of doctrine for understanding difficult passages, God calls us to defend what we believe. In the passage we are studying (1 Peter 3:8-22), Peter again speaks of the abuse Christians will suffer within a world that wants to forget God. It is in this context of suffering for Jesus that he says, "Always be prepared to make a defense to any one who calls you to account for the hope that is in you, yet do it with gentleness and reverence" (verse 15, RSV).

Proper understanding of the doctrines will make the defense of our faith clear to those who demand such a defense. It is our doctrinal position that makes Seventh-day Adventists different from other religious bodies that claim the name of Jesus. As Ellen White says, "Seventh-day Adventists have been chosen by God as a peculiar people, separate from the world." And what makes Seventh-day Adventists unique? It is the body of truth that has been committed to us—our doctrines. "The greatest wealth of truth ever entrusted to mortals, the most solemn and fearful warnings ever sent by God to man, have been committed to them to be given to the world."[7]

Because of the precious gift of biblical truth that has been given to this church, we can confidently defend our faith and our hope with all gentleness and reverence.

Summary

We have seen how a correct doctrinal understanding helps to interpret two very difficult passages of Scripture relating to the state of the dead (1 Peter 3:19, 20; Philippians 1:23). Although some may think the study of doctrine is as dry as the dust of Babylon, doctrines are important. They are the foundation of religious belief and the precious gift of truth given by God to His people.

---

1. Charles Biggs, *A Critical and Exegetical Commentary of the Epistles of St. Peter and St. Jude* (Edinburgh: T & T Clark, 1978), p. 162.

2. *Selected Messages*, bk. 2, p. 58.

3. *The Great Controversy*, p. 588.

4. "Adventists and the Sabbath," transcript of audio tape by Dr. Walter Martin, March 15, 1989, Fresno, Calif.

5. *Seventh-day Adventist Bible Commentary*, vol. 1, p. 1088.

6. Ibid., pp. 1088, 1089.

7. *Testimonies for the Church*, vol. 7, p. 138.

Chapter 11
Victory and Service

1 Peter 4:1-11

In the previous chapter, we noted Peter's comment that Paul's writings contain "some things hard to be understood" (2 Peter 3:16). We have discovered, however, that Peter himself was capable of writing some things that are also hard to understand. The first verse of chapter 4 presents another difficult statement.

Suffer and Stop Sinning

Peter returns to the topic of suffering by saying, "Forasmuch then as Christ hath suffered for us in the flesh, arm yourselves likewise with the same mind: for he that hath suffered in the flesh hath ceased from sin" (1 Peter 4:1). Before we turn our attention to the concluding statement in this verse, it might be helpful to summarize what Peter says about suffering.

This topic is introduced at four different points in Peter's epistle. Each time the context differs, but Peter always refers to Jesus as the example of how to deal with suffering. First, he addresses servants who suffer abuse at the hands of unjust masters (2:18-25). Then he admonishes all Christians who may suffer for righteousness' sake not to retaliate (3:13-18). In our passage for this chapter (4:1-11), Peter returns a third time to the topic of suffering. We will see shortly that 4:1-6 is a continuation of 3:13-18. Peter's discussion of suffering in 3:13-18 was interrupted by his digression on the spirits in prison. Finally, he returns to suffering for the fourth time in 4:12-19, where he exhorts Christians to hold up under abuse, because if they are reproached for the gospel of Christ, they will be blessed.

Now we must return to the question raised by Peter's comment in 4:1. How are we to understand the statement that the person who suffers in the flesh no longer sins? This verse can be understood properly only when it is placed alongside of 3:18. When this is done, it becomes clear that the discussion about Jesus preaching to the spirits in prison is parenthetical, and 4:1 is a continuation of the thought that Peter was developing earlier.

Let us put 3:18 and 4:1 side by side and look for a logical flow of thought:

> Christ also hath once suffered for sins, the just for the unjust, that he might bring us to God, being put to death in the flesh, but quickened by the Spirit [3:18]; . . . forasmuch then as Christ hath suffered for us in the flesh, arm yourselves likewise with the same mind: for he that hath suffered in the flesh hath ceased from sin [4:1].

Two concepts in these two verses must be examined: (1) the solidarity that exists between the suffering of Christ and His followers and (2) the cessation from sin.

1. *Solidarity with Christ.* The suffering that Jesus endured was for our sins, the just for the unjust. His suffering included not only verbal and physical abuse, but death. The New Testament includes the concept that those who accept Jesus as their Saviour enter into His suffering and death. This concept can be described as solidarity on the part of the repentant sinner and

VICTORY AND SERVICE 101

his Lord—a shared identity, a corporate experience.

Peter says, "Arm yourselves likewise with the same mind." The apostle Paul gives a similar admonition,

> Let this mind be in you, which was also in Christ Jesus: who, being in the form of God, thought it not robbery to be equal with God: but made himself of no reputation, and took upon him the form of a servant, and was made in the likeness of men: and being found in fashion as a man, he humbled himself, and became obedient unto death, even the death of the cross (Philippians 2:5-8).

That death is our death.

2. *Cessation from sin.* Having described the believer as having entered into the experience of suffering and death to sin in solidarity with Jesus, Peter then says, "He that hath suffered in the flesh hath ceased from sin." Peter is not saying that physical suffering for the cause of Christ automatically absolves us from all sin. Rather, he suggests that we suffer corporately in Christ's suffering and that we die corporately in Christ's death. Because Jesus died once for all for sins (3:18), when we accept Him, we die to sin in solidarity with Him.

The apostle Paul expresses the concept of corporate life and death in Christ this way:

> What shall we say then? Shall we continue in sin, that grace may abound? God forbid. How shall we, that are dead to sin, live any longer therein? Know ye not, that so many of us as were baptized into Jesus Christ were baptized into his death? Therefore we are buried with him by baptism into death: that like as Christ was raised up from the dead by the glory of the Father, even so we also should walk in newness of life. For if we have been planted together in the likeness of his death, we shall be also in the likeness of his resurrection: knowing this, that our old man is crucified with him, that the body of sin might be destroyed, that henceforth we should not

serve sin. For he that is dead is freed from sin (Romans 6:1-7).

Commenting on the solidarity between Jesus and His people, Alan M. Stibbs says:

> What is here inculcated is more than *imitatio Christi*, or the following of Christ's example. It is rather *unio mystica* or mystical union, a sense of dying with Christ to sin and of raising in Him to a new life which is to be lived for God. It is noteworthy, too, what importance is attached (both here and elsewhere in the New Testament) to a new and right attitude of mind as being fundamental to that radical change of behavior which ought to express itself in the lives of all who belong to Christ.[1]

Victory Over Sin

Being dead to sin because of our solidarity with Jesus in His suffering and death leads Peter to emphasize once again that victory over sin can now be a reality in the life of every Christian:

> So as to live for the rest of the time in the flesh no longer by human passions but by the will of God. Let the time that is past suffice for doing what the Gentiles like to do, living in licentiousness, passions, drunkenness, revels, carousing, and lawless idolatry. They are surprised that you do not now join them in the same wild profligacy, and they abuse you (verses 2-4, RSV).

But victory over the old lifestyle and old habits does not come easily. Ellen White says, "The warfare against self is the greatest battle that was ever fought. The yielding of self, surrendering all to the will of God, requires a struggle; but the soul must submit to God before it can be renewed in holiness."[2] The good news is that we do not have to go through this struggle alone. When we are willing to enter into solidarity with Jesus' suffering and death, we are kept by Him, and

VICTORY AND SERVICE 103

Satan cannot touch us. This is the assurance that John gives us: "We know that any one born of God does not sin, but he who was born of God [Jesus] keeps him, and the evil one does not touch him" (1 John 5:18, RSV).

Paul talks in terms of Christians being co-workers with Jesus in their own salvation: "Wherefore, my beloved, as ye have always obeyed, not as in my presence only, but now much more in my absence, work out your own salvation with fear and trembling." Then the apostle hastens on to point out that this work is a joint venture: "It is God which worketh in you both to will and to do of his good pleasure" (Philippians 2:12, 13).

The surrender of the will to God, which is the right action of the will, coupled with God's working out His will within us, places us in the position of being co-workers with Him in our own salvation. On the basis of this relationship, John could say that those who are born of God do not sin because Jesus keeps them, and the devil cannot touch them. But if this relationship is broken, the Christian becomes fair game for the predator for human souls.

How crucial is the right action of the will—the surrendering of the will to God? We have an illustration of its importance in the story of the rich young man who asked Jesus what he must do to have eternal life. Jesus told him to sell all that he had, give to the poor, and follow Him. Jesus could say nothing else, do nothing more for the young man. All Jesus could do was to stand there and watch "the greatest battle that was ever fought" rage within the heart of this man. He would not interfere with the responsibility that God has given to each one of us—the exercise of the will. Finally the young man made a decision, exercised his free will, and turned his back and walked away from the only One who could give him eternal life; and Jesus did nothing to stop him.

The right exercise of the will is the surrender of the will to God; only then will the fallen human nature be brought under control. "You can give Him your will; He will then work in you to will and to do according to His good pleasure. Thus your whole nature will be brought under the control of the Spirit of

Christ."[3] At this point, victory over temptation and sin becomes a reality—and remains a reality as long as the Spirit of Christ is allowed to control the fallen nature.

Judgment

As Peter speaks of the lifestyle of the Gentiles (verses 3, 4), he raises more questions: "Who shall give account to him that is ready to judge the quick and the dead. For this cause was the gospel preached also to them that are dead, that they might be judged according to men in the flesh, but live according to God in the spirit" (1 Peter 4:5, 6). Two questions immediately come to mind: (1) who are the dead who heard the gospel? and (2) what is the nature of the judgment referred to?

The dead. Those who defend the idea that Jesus preached to the spirits in the prison house of death between His crucifixion and resurrection use this verse in an attempt to strengthen their position. On the basis of the New Testament doctrine of death being an unconscious sleep, it is impossible for those who have died to hear the gospel once their life here on earth is over. Peter is evidently talking about people who heard the gospel preached but died before Peter wrote his epistle.

The judgment. All Christians accept the biblical teaching that those who choose to remain in sin and rebellion against their Creator and Redeemer must be punished—thus the need for a judgment. Only a few, however, accept the concept of another phase of judgment prior to the destruction of evil. Seventh-day Adventists are among the few who believe that the Bible teaches an investigative or pre-advent judgment. Peter's statement on judgment in verse 5 may be seen as referring to: (1) the investigative phase of judgment, (2) the executive phase, or (3) both investigation and execution. The reference to judgment in verse 6 will be dealt with separately.

I believe that verse 5 must be understood as referring to an investigative phase. The pre-advent, investigative judgment is understood by Seventh-day Adventists to be an experience of rendering accounts. In this judgment, those who have had and still maintain a saved relationship with Jesus are vindicated.

Those who have not maintained a saved relationship are judged as unworthy.

In addition, there is a second investigative phase. Those who have heard the gospel and have witnessed it in the lives of Jesus' followers but have rejected it, as seems to be the case of the Gentiles Peter refers to in verses 3-5, must assume the responsibility for their decisions and also render an account. This accounting takes place in the pre-white-throne judgment period during the millennium (see Revelation 20:4).

The idea of rendering an account under an investigation is present in several of Jesus' parables. For example, the unforgiving servant (Matthew 18:23-35), the marriage feast (Matthew 22:1-14; Luke 14:15-24), the faithful servant (Matthew 24:45-51; Luke 12:41-48), the talents (Matthew 25:14-30; Luke 19:11-27), and judgment of the nations (Matthew 25:31-46).

The scene in Daniel 7, where judgment is rendered in favor of God's people, is, perhaps, the best-known passage on the investigative judgment. Hebrews contains another that is not as well known as the one in Daniel, and, like the parables of Jesus, deals with the rendering of accounts. Before looking at this passage, however, we must note two things about the book of Hebrews: (1) The flow of thought is always from the lesser to the greater, from the known to the unknown; this fact must be especially noted in dealing with the heavenly sanctuary and the high priestly work of Jesus. (2) The book contains five sections, each subdivided into three parts that always appear in the same sequence—theological argument, warning, and statement of judgment.[4]

In the judgment section (Hebrews 10:28-39) of the fourth division (6:9–10:39), a pre-advent, investigative judgment is clearly taught:

> A man who has violated the law of Moses dies without mercy at the testimony of two or three witnesses. How much worse punishment do you think will be deserved by the man who has spurned the Son of God, and profaned the blood of the covenant by which he was sanctified, and outraged the Spirit of grace? (10:28, 29, RSV).

Remembering the literary method of moving from the lesser to the greater, we can see that a heavenly investigative judgment is taught. First, the familiar investigative procedures in an earthly trial are introduced. In the earthly court of law, two or three witnesses present the evidence against the individual who is accused of violating the law of Moses. On the basis of the evidence presented, the accused is found guilty and then punished.

Then the scene moves from the lesser to the greater, from the known to the unknown, from an earthly investigative trial to the heavenly investigative trial. This movement can be seen in the words, "How much worse punishment do you think will be deserved by the man . . ." (verse 29, RSV). In the heavenly court scene, witnesses bear testimony against the accused, just as in the earthly court. There are three of them, just as the Mosaic law requires for a verdict. The witnesses are three facts that bear their testimony. The accused has (1) spurned the Son of God, (2) profaned the blood of the covenant by which he was sanctified, and (3) outraged the Spirit of grace. These Scriptures present enough evidence to convince me of a pre-advent, investigative judgment.

In 1 Peter 4:6, we see another reference to investigation, but this time not in the context of the heavenly investigative judgment. This judgment is mentioned briefly to prevent confusion between the judgments spoken of in verses 5 and 6. Verse 6 tells that the dead had the gospel preached to them, "that they might be judged according (*kata*) to men in the flesh, but live according (*kata*) to God in the spirit." The Greek preposition *kata*, when used with the accusative case of reference, introduces the idea of a standard or rule of measurement.[5]

Peter suggests that the dead who had heard the gospel were judged by the Gentiles on the basis of their standard of measurement. In verse 4, Peter has already pointed out that the followers of Jesus are considered peculiar and are abused because they do not join the Gentiles in their riotous living. Peter then goes on to say that although the followers of Jesus are judged peculiar by human standards, they are actually living according to God's standards. Let's look at a loose paraphrase of verse 6 in an attempt to reveal the nuances: "Because, on this account, the gospel was even preached to those who have died, with the result that they are judged according to the standards of men with respect to the flesh, but they live according to the standards of God with respect to the spirit."

Summary

The good news of the gospel is that through our solidarity with Jesus, we die to sin and are raised to a new life in Him through His death for sin and His resurrection. Therefore, our fallen, sinful natures, now under the control of the Holy Spirit, will not dominate our words, acts, and thoughts. The old lifestyle (the old man of sin) has died; it has been set aside. Therefore, the pre-advent, investigative judgment becomes a vindication and reverses the negative judgment that has been passed upon God's people by people who use their own standards of measurement.

---

1. Alan Stibbs, *The First Epistle General of Peter* (Grand Rapids: Wm. B. Eerdmans Publishing Company, 1971), p. 148.

2. *Steps to Christ*, p. 43.

3. Ibid., p. 47.

4. George E. Rice, "Apostasy as a Motif and Its Effect on the Structure of Hebrews," *Andrews Seminary Studies*, vol. 23 (Spring 1985), pp. 29-35.

5. James A. Brooks and Carlton L. Winbery, *Syntax of New Testament Greek* (Washington, D.C.: University Press of America, Inc., 1979), p. 51.

Chapter 12
Suffering and the Christian

1 Peter 4:12-19

The Christian is no stranger to suffering. But only as we understand the great controversy and its implications for the followers of Jesus does suffering become comprehensible. While those who know nothing of the spiritual warfare swirling around them cannot understand why the good suffer, Christians who do know about the battle between good and evil understand why suffering and trials are a part of life. They can also look with confidence in their Redeemer to a better day when pain and suffering, along with the originator of all misery, will be eliminated.

In the last half of chapter 4, Peter returns to the problem of suffering. Although he has addressed this issue in previous chapters, he now places suffering in a context that differs from the earlier discussions. He speaks of suffering in terms of "the fiery ordeal" (RSV) and connects it with the revealing of Jesus' glory and judgment. In other words, Peter addresses suffering within the context of the climactic events of the great controversy.

Wrath of the Dragon

Peter says, "Beloved, think it not strange concerning the fiery trial which is to try you, as though some strange thing happened unto you" (1 Peter 4:12). With the use of the Greek futuristic present tense, Peter speaks of the fiery trial as still in the future, but its certainty is as real as though it were already present.

If the reader is not aware of the great controversy theme that runs through Scripture, he will probably overlook the reference to a fiery trial awaiting God's people in connection with a revelation of Jesus' glory and judgment. But to the one who is aware of this theme, Peter's words take on meaning in light of Revelation 12—the chapter that opens up the subject of the great controversy.

In this chapter, Satan is portrayed as a dragon who, with his evil angels, began a war in heaven and was cast out into the earth (Revelation 12:7-9). The intensity with which the dragon presses the conflict on our planet is reflected in the woe pronounced upon those who dwell on earth: "Woe to the inhabiters of the earth and of the sea! for the devil is come down unto you, having great wrath, because he knoweth that he hath but a short time" (verse 12).

His deadly anger is portrayed by three violent confrontations here on earth. (1) Standing before the woman (God's people) who is about to give birth, he is prepared to destroy her Child as soon as He is born (verses 3-5). (2) When unsuccessful in his first confrontation, he violently turns upon the woman in an attempt to destroy her (verses 13-16). (3) Failing the second time, he then vents his anger upon the descendants of the woman who keep the commandments of God and have the testimony of Jesus (verse 17). Except for his attempt to destroy the Child, Satan's wrath is poured upon a people. This point deserves further study.

God Has a People

Prior to the Exodus, God was represented upon earth by individuals. From Adam to Jacob we do not read of a people

SUFFERING AND THE CHRISTIAN 111

that God called His own, but only of individuals and members of their families. With the call of Abraham, however, God began building a nation to exist among nations as His people. But not until Egyptian bondage and the Exodus did this nation emerge as an identifiable entity.

God said to Israel, "Thou art an holy people unto the Lord thy God: the Lord thy God hath chosen thee to be a special people unto himself, above all people that are upon the face of the earth" (Deuteronomy 7:6). God then clearly laid out the reasons why He had chosen Israel: (1) "Because he would keep the oath which he had sworn unto your fathers. . . . Know therefore that the Lord thy God, he is God, the faithful God, which keepeth covenant and mercy with them that love him and keep his commandments." (2) "Thou shalt therefore keep the commandments, and the statutes, and the judgments, which I command thee this day, to do them" (verses 8, 9, 11).

From that moment on, God's people were identified by: (1) their solidarity, their corporate identity with Abraham—the patriarch with whom God had established His covenant, and (2) their willingness to accept and preserve a body of truth, the foundation of which is the law of God. Paul speaks of this law, which includes the statutes and judgments spoken of in Deuteronomy, as "the embodiment of knowledge and truth" (Romans 2:20, RSV).

By the time Jesus ministered on earth, the covenant relationship established during Moses' ministry had soured to the point where the covenant people did not recognize the covenant God when He appeared to them, and they put Him to death.

At the conclusion of his Pentecost speech, Peter laid out two profound concepts before the covenant people. As he exhorted them to accept Jesus and to be baptized, he said, "The promise is unto you, and to your children, and to all that are afar off. . . . Save yourself from this untoward [crooked, RSV] generation" (Acts 2:39, 40). First, Peter told the Jews that non-Jews were to share in the covenant promises that God had given to them. Second, he warned the people that something was about to happen to the people who had rejected the covenant of God, and that they had better separate themselves from that people.

Peter's warning is clarified in the next speech:

> Moses truly said unto the fathers, A prophet shall the Lord your God raise up unto you of your brethren, like unto me; him shall ye hear in all things whatsoever he shall say unto you. And it shall come to pass, that every soul, which will not hear that prophet, shall be destroyed [Greek, *exolethreuō*] from among the people (Acts 3:22, 23).

The prophet that Moses spoke of in Deuteronomy is Jesus, but Peter gives this quotation different application. Rather than being "destroyed from among the people" for rejecting Jesus, God said to Moses, "I will require it of him" (Deuteronomy 18:19). Where did Peter get the idea that those who rejected the Prophet that Moses spoke of will be destroyed from among the covenant people? The idea comes from the covenant itself that God made with Abraham.

As God established His covenant with Abraham, He said that those who break the covenant will be "cut off [*exolethreuō*] from his people" (Genesis 17:14). Peter borrowed this one word from the Septuagint translation of Genesis to conclude his quotation of Deuteronomy. He wanted his reader to understand that the person who is guilty of breaking the covenant will be cut off or destroyed from among the covenant people.

Some who listened to Peter's speech heeded the warning. They separated themselves from the crooked generation that brought about Jesus' death, accepted Jesus as their Saviour, and escaped being cut off from the covenant people. This is Paul's point as he discusses the condition of his fellow countrymen:

> They are Israelites, and to them belong the sonship, the glory, the covenants, the giving of the law, the worship, and the promises; to them belong the patriarchs, and of their race, according to the flesh, is the Christ.

SUFFERING AND THE CHRISTIAN 113

God who is over all be blessed for ever. Amen.
But it is not as though the word of God had failed. For not all who are descended from Israel belong to Israel, and not all are children of Abraham because they are his descendants; but "Through Isaac shall your descendants be named." This means that it is not the children of the flesh who are the children of God, but the children of the promise are reckoned as descendants (Romans 9:4-8, RSV).

Paul continues by asking,

Has God rejected his people? By no means! I myself am an Israelite, a descendant of Abraham, a member of the tribe of Benjamin. God has not rejected his people whom he foreknew. . . . What then? Israel failed to obtain what it sought. The elect obtained it, but the rest were hardened (Romans 11:1, 2, 7, RSV).

Those who rejected Jesus, those who were hardened, were cut off [*exolethreuō*] from the covenant. But to the original Jewish followers of Jesus were now added Gentile converts. But two qualifications for the covenant relationship still remained: (1) solidarity with Abraham and (2) willingness to embrace God's law, which is the embodiment of truth. How do these two qualifications apply after the cross?

1. Solidarity with Abraham was no longer by natural descent. This solidarity is now based upon the acceptance of Jesus, because, according to Paul, the fulfillment of the covenant promises made to Abraham were realized by Jesus and then shared with those who accept Him: "Now to Abraham and his seed were the promises made. He saith not, And to seeds, as of many; but as of one, And to thy seed, which is Christ" (Galatians 3:16). For this reason, those who accept Christ are considered descendants of Abraham and qualify to receive the benefits of the Abrahamic covenant: "Know ye therefore that they which are of faith, the same are the children of Abraham." "And if ye be Christ's, then are ye Abraham's seed, and heirs

according to the promise" (verses 7, 29).

2. Those who accept Jesus necessarily accept His gospel, which not only includes God's law but amplifies it. Therefore, accepting the gospel fulfills the requirement of accepting the law.

Thus from the apostles onward, God's covenant people continue to exist. Even at the end of time a remnant is identified. They, too, fulfill the two qualifications that make them God's covenant people. First of all, they are identified as the remnant of the seed of the woman (Revelation 12:17). The woman represents Christ's followers that preceded them; therefore, they are believers in Jesus. This is the basis of their solidarity with Abraham. The second qualification is also stated in verse 17. They "keep the commandments of God, and have the testimony of Jesus Christ." They not only possess a body of truth (the testimony of Jesus), but they accept and keep the commandments of God that are contained in and amplified by this body of truth.

On this point Ellen White says: "Seventh-day Adventists have been chosen by God as a peculiar people, separate from the world. . . . The greatest wealth of truth ever entrusted to mortals, the most solemn and fearful warnings ever sent by God to man, have been committed to them to be given to the world."[1]

According to John in Revelation 12, the dragon turns his anger upon the woman and the remnant of her seed when he fails to destroy the man child. It is the unleashing of this wrath by the dragon that Peter refers to as the fiery ordeal (RSV) that is to come upon the followers of Jesus. Although the original readers of Peter's epistle were soon to experience persecution and fiery ordeals, the wrath of the dragon is to become especially hot against the remnant of the woman's seed when the time arrives for judgment and the revelation of Jesus' glory.

Time for Judgment

For the second time in chapter 4, Peter raises the issue of judgment by saying, "The time is come that judgment must begin at the house of God: and if it first begin at us, what shall the end be of them that obey not the gospel of God?" (verse 17). In this verse judgment is set in the context of the fiery ordeal that God's people will suffer and the revealing of Jesus' glory. As we have already seen, this context suggests the end-time events. But which judgment is Peter speaking of—the investigative judgment or the execution of the verdict? Is it possible that Peter uses the term *judgment* as an umbrella to cover both phases of judgment and the eschatological events related to them?

Many commentators say that Peter appeals to a concept of judgment that is firmly established in Jewish thinking—all judgment begins with God's people to purify them, and then it moves to God's enemies. By saying that judgment begins at the house of God, Peter is alluding to Ezekiel 9. In this chapter, a man with a writer's inkhorn at his side is commanded to mark all who sigh and cry for the abominations done in the midst of Jerusalem. When his work is finished, God commands others to slay those who did not receive the mark—both old and young, men, women, and children—and the work of slaughter is to begin at the sanctuary, the house of God. In Ezekiel 9, those slain are in a state of incurable rebellion.

It would appear that this chapter in Ezekiel presents a two-phase judgment: (1) an investigation of all who claim to be God's people, which results in the marking of those whom God considers as His, and (2) the execution of those who failed the investigation—beginning at the house of God.

Simon J. Kistemaker notes the difference between the people in Ezekiel's vision and Peter's readers:

> By contrast, the recipients of Peter's epistle, who also are God's elect (1:1), endure suffering for the sake of Christ. For this reason, Peter calls them blessed (verse 14). These people receive God's judgment not in the form of condemnation but in the name of Christ as exoneration.[2]

Kistemaker's idea of exoneration is similar to the Seventh-day Adventist point of view: God's people will be exonerated in judgment, while those who have rejected God's mercy receive condemnation and punishment. Kistemaker, however, sees exoneration at the time of the executive judgment, while Seventh-day Adventists see the exoneration of God's people in both phases of judgment—investigation and execution.

Ellen White applies 1 Peter 4:17 to the investigative judgment by tying it to the typical service of the Day of Atonement. She then points out that the wicked are also judged, but in a separate work that takes place at a later time.[3] So it is that "judgment must begin at the house of God: and if it first begin at us, what shall the end be of them that obey not the gospel?" (1 Peter 4:17).

A further point is worthy of note here. Kistemaker translates the first part of verse 17 as follows: "For it is time for judgment to begin with the family of God." *Family* or *household* (RSV) is a legitimate translation of the word that appears as *house* in the KJV. The context of the verse supports the interpretation that Peter is not thinking of the heavenly sanctuary per se (*house*), but, rather, God's people, for he does say in the next clause, "And if it first begins at us." The judgment then moves "from" God's people or family who are exonerated in the judgment "to" those who refuse to obey and are condemned in judgment.[4]

As Peter penned these words on judgment, it is possible that he had both the investigative and the executive phases of judgment in mind. The allusion to Ezekiel 9 can suggest both. The investigative phase can be suggested in the idea that judgment begins with God's people and then moves to those who reject Him, as Ellen White applies the verse in *The Great Controversy*. On the other hand, if Peter is reflecting his Jewish background, the suffering to be endured by his readers could have been thought to be the cleansing of God's people that precedes God's judgments upon those who reject the gospel of Jesus.

Summary

God's unique people are identified by two characteristics: (1) solidarity with Abraham through their belief in Jesus

Christ and (2) acceptance of a body of truth that is based upon God's ten-commandment law. This people, and especially those at the end of time, are the subjects of Satan's wrath. In the context of the struggle between good and evil Peter again turns to the issue of suffering. This, in turn, leads Peter to a second statement about judgment that appears to be broad enough to encompass its two phases—investigative and executive. Peter emphasizes the solemnity of the times by telling his readers that judgment is to begin with them.

---

1. *Testimonies for the Church*, vol. 7, p. 138.
2. Simon J. Kistemaker, *Exposition of the Epistles of Peter and of the Epistle of Jude* (Grand Rapids: Baker Book House, 1987), p. 180.
3. *The Great Controversy*, p. 480.
4. Kistemaker, p. 180.

Chapter 13
Final Exhortations

1 Peter 5:1-14

Memories of Jesus filled the minds of the apostles and affected everything they did. Peter, James, and John had the unique privilege of being the closest to Jesus during His earthly ministry. Try to grasp what it must have been like to live with God, to eat with Him, to talk with Him, to question Him and listen to His answers, and to share the common things of life with Him—His days, His nights, His work, His interests in people, His concerns, and His frustrations. Try to imagine what it must have been like to touch Him, to look into His eyes, to feel His hand upon your shoulder, and to hear His words of encouragement.

The apostle John marvels over the entire experience:

> That which was from the beginning, which we have heard, which we have seen with our eyes, which we have looked upon, and our hands have handled, of the Word of life; (for the life was manifested, and we have seen it, and bear witness, and shew unto you that eternal life, which was with the Father, and was manifested unto us;)

that which we have seen and heard declare we unto you, that ye also may have fellowship with us: and truly our fellowship is with the Father, and with his Son Jesus Christ. And these things we write unto you, that your joy may be full (1 John 1:1-4).

Peter, too, recaptures the past as he brings his epistle to its close. Three experiences stand out in his memory: (1) the suffering of Jesus that he witnessed from Caiaphas's courtyard (1 Peter 5:1), (2) the glory that Jesus shared with James and John on the Mount of Transfiguration (verse 1), and (3) the restoration to his former position as an apostle (verse 2).

As Peter closes his epistle, his mind drifts back through the years to that early morning when Jesus met seven of His disciples on the shore of Galilee after a night of fishing (John 21:1-17). Speaking to Peter, Jesus says, "Simon, son of Jonas, lovest thou me?" Peter replies, "Yea, Lord; thou knowest that I love thee." He never forgot the response of the Good Shepherd: "Feed my sheep" (John 21:16).

Now, many years later, Peter passes on the charge of the Good Shepherd to those who are called by God to be undershepherds—"Feed the flock of God which is among you" (1 Peter 5:2).

Elders, Feed the Flock

When Jesus recommissioned Peter as an apostle, He charged him with two responsibilities: (1) to feed (*boskō*) His sheep and lambs (1 John 21:15, 17) and (2) to shepherd (*poimainō*) His sheep (verse 16). The word used in John 21:15 and 17 means "to provide with nourishment." Thus Peter was to provide food for Jesus' flock. In verse 16, Peter is charged with the further responsibility of shepherding. "To shepherd" pictures a broader function than the word used in verses 15 and 17, and it means to care for a flock, which, of course, would include the provision of food.

In this commission, Jesus is charging Peter with the responsibility of providing mature Christians with proper food from God's Word, while tenderly caring for the lambs and seeing that they also are properly fed. The lambs may be our children who are growing into a knowledge of God as they follow the example of their parents and their elders in the church. The lambs could also be new members who need the nurturing and loving concern of those who are more mature in Christ.

Whether they are sheep or lambs, all must be properly fed. The sheep need a diet of solid food from the Word, while the lambs need milk to encourage their development. Paul says, "Every one who lives on milk is unskilled in the word of righteousness, for he is a child. But solid food is for the mature, for those who have their faculties trained by practice to distinguish good from evil" (Hebrews 5:13, 14, RSV). To feed the sheep milk will weaken them. To feed the lambs solid food will give them spiritual indigestion. A wise undershepherd will know what to feed to whom.

A Matter of Motives

Not only are the spiritual guardians of God's people to tend the flock, but they are also to examine their own motives in assuming such responsibility. Ellen White recognizes that not every person denominationally ordained has been chosen by God for the work of an undershepherd. In a statement that deserves the prayerful consideration of every person asked to accept the responsibility of spiritual leadership, Ellen White says:

> Some have entered the work with a human commission rather than the divine. They have educated themselves as debaters, and the churches under their care show the character of their work. They were not ready, they were not fitted for the work. Their hearts are not right with God. In short, they have a theory but not true conversion and sanctification through the truth.

The next sentence should cause all spiritual leaders in God's cause to pause and reexamine their motives: "The great issue so near at hand [national Sunday law] will weed out those whom God has not appointed, and He will have a pure, true, sanctified ministry prepared for the latter rain."[1]

Ellen White and Peter shared the same concern—that spiritual leaders have the right motives for accepting responsibility. Peter puts forward three negative and three positive motives for the consideration of church leaders. The negatives are (1) not by constraint, (2) not for filthy lucre, and (3) neither as being lords over God's heritage. Each negative motive has a corresponding positive motive: (1) but willingly, (2) but of a ready mind, and (3) but being examples to the flock (verses 2, 3).

Constraint. Some accept positions of spiritual leadership that conflict with their personal preference. They accept or train for spiritual leadership because an authority figure in their lives persuaded them to be a pastor or elder. Coercion of any kind is the wrong motive for being in a position of spiritual leadership. Peter says that these responsibilities must be taken up willingly.

Filthy lucre. Greed and the desire for personal ease has motivated some toward spiritual leadership. Sometimes a pleasing personality and charm have been used in a spiritual setting to take advantage of the flock. The spirit of such religious leaders is totally foreign to the spirit of self-sacrifice that brought God's Son to earth to die for our sinful race.

The Greek word translated *filthy lucre* (KJV) or *shameful gain* (RSV) in verse 2 depicts a "mean man" (*aischrokerdōs*).

> The mean man is he who never sets enough food before his guests and who gives himself a double portion when he is carving the joint. He waters the wine; he goes to the theatre only when he can get a free ticket. He never has enough money to pay the fare and always borrows from his fellow-passengers. When he is selling corn, he uses a measure in which the bottom is pushed up, and even then he carefully levels the top. He counts the half radishes left over from dinner in case the servants eat any. Rather than give a wedding present, he will go away

from home when a wedding is in the offing.[2]

But Peter says that elders are to serve with a ready mind (KJV) or eagerly (RSV). The prospect for personal gain should not determine whether one will serve.

Lords over God's heritage. Lust for power is just as dangerous to the flock as is greed. Jesus warned the disciples against the thirst for power:

> Ye know that the princes of the Gentiles exercise dominion over them, and they that are great exercise authority upon them. But it shall not be so among you: but whosoever will be great among you, let him be your minister; and whosoever will be chief among you, let him be your servant: even as the Son of man came not to be ministered unto, but to minister, and to give his life a ransom for many (Matthew 20:25-28).

Ellen White warns leadership, "Let no one suppose that God has given to men the power of ruling their fellow-men. He will accept the service of no man who hurts and discourages Christ's heritage."[3] In contrast to lording it over the flock, Peter advises, be "ensamples to the flock" (5:3).

Of Crowns and Things

Peter assures the elders that if they remain faithful undershepherds and serve from proper motives, "When the chief Shepherd shall appear, ye shall receive a crown of glory that fadeth not away" (1 Peter 5:4). The crown (*stephanos*, from which we derive the Christian name Stephen) spoken of here is a symbol of victory. In Peter's time, it was made out of pine boughs, celery leaves, rose petals, and a variety of other plant material. The crown of thorns that Jesus wore was a *stephanos* (Matthew 27:29).

The word *stephanos* can also mean "an award." Paul used this meaning in Philippians 4:1, where he calls the members of this church his joy and his crown; they have been awarded to him as a result of his labor in preaching the gospel in their city. He also calls the Thessalonian Christians his "crown of rejoicing" (1 Thessalonians 2:19). We can also understand the "crown of righteousness" (2 Timothy 4:8) and the "crown of life" (Revelation 2:10) as being the awards given by Jesus to His people, and not as an ornament to be worn upon the head.

A second type of crown is mentioned in the New Testament. The *diadēma*, from which we get the English word *diadem*, is a symbol of kingly power. Introduced by the Persians kings, it was a blue ribbon embroidered with white designs. According to 1 Maccabees 11:13, when Ptolemy of Egypt conquered the rival capital of the Seleucids, he rode into Antioch wearing two "crowns" (*diadēmata*, blue ribbons), one symbolized his lordship over Egypt, and the other, his newly acquired lordship over "Asia."

The great red dragon of Revelation 12:3 wears a blue ribbon on each of its seven heads as do the ten horns of the beast of Revelation 13:1. These blue ribbons indicate that the heads and horns are political powers. Understanding that a *diadēma* is a blue ribbon helps to explain Revelation 19:12, where Christ, riding on a white horse, wears many crowns (*diadēmata*), for He is "King of kings, and Lord of lords" (verse 16).

The "crown [*stephanos*] of glory" that Peter speaks of in verse 4 can be understood either as the glory awarded to the redeemed and shared with Jesus in His kingdom or as a verbal description of the crown given to the redeemed at Jesus' return, i.e., a glorious crown.

Roaring Lion

Near the close of his letter, Peter returns to the great controversy theme that he introduced in chapter 4: "Be sober, be vigilant; because your adversary the devil, as a roaring lion, walketh about, seeking whom he may devour: whom resist steadfast in the faith, knowing that the same afflictions are accomplished in your brethren that are in the world" (1 Peter 5:8, 9).

I have heard it said that the lion roars only during the hunt. I am afraid that as individual Christians, we tend to

FINAL EXHORTATIONS 125

minimize the fact that Satan is on the h[...] The intensity with which the destroyer carries out [...] on is treated as some trifling thing, as somethin[...] only passing notice. Ellen White tries to aro[...] danger we are in: "Satan is earnest and sincere [...] He was once an honored angel in heaven, and [...] as lost his holiness, he has not lost his power. [...] ower with terrible effect. He does not wait for h[...] to him. He hunts for it."[4]

We cannot resist the devil one-on-one; his pow[...] at for us. He has defeated humanity, and when we [...] d up against him in our own strength, we lose every [...] ut he can be beaten if we are willing to do two things: (1) [...] to Jesus for divine help, and (2) use this help to resist the devil's advances.

Divine help. Divine help is offered to every tempted soul who is willing to accept it. Although humanity was overcome by the enemy, Jesus engaged him on his own ground and defeated him. The power that gained the victory is offered to us. Consider the following promises: (1) " 'Resist the devil,' and the promise is, 'he will flee from you.' Why? Because the angel of God lifts up for you a standard against the enemy, and he flees."[5] (2) "When we come to God in sincerity, and give ourselves to Him, He will strengthen us to stand against the wiles of the enemy. In the power of Jesus Christ, resist the enemy, and he will flee from you."[6] (3) "Satan trembles and flees before the weakest soul who finds refuge in that mighty name."[7]

If we take the issues in the great controversy lightly, we will not feel the urgency in going to God in complete surrender and finding the power that will repel Satan. If we are overcome, we have only ourselves to blame.

Resistance. We must be energetic if we are to be victorious over temptation. God provides the power, but we must put forth the effort to call upon it and use it. Ellen White laments over the lethargy among God's professed people in obtaining the promised help: "Without divine help they will be unable to control human passions and appetites. In Christ is the very

126 A LIVING HOPE

help needed, but how few will come to Him for that help."[8]

As the devil is in dead earnest about his role in the great controversy, so the follower of Jesus is to be in dead earnest about obtaining help in his warfare against temptation and sin. To vacillate in the heat of battle will eventually lead to the loss of the war. "Purity of life and a character molded after the divine Pattern are not obtained without earnest effort and fixed principles. A vacillating person will not succeed in attaining Christian perfection."[9]

Tenacious resistance in the power of Jesus is the only answer to the sins that beset us:

> Our only safety is in giving no place to the devil; for his suggestions and purposes are ever to injure us, and hinder us from relying upon God. He transforms himself into an angel of purity, that he may, through his specious temptations, introduce his devices in such a manner that we may not discern his wiles. The more we yield, the more powerful will be his deceptions over us. It is unsafe to controvert or to parley with him. For every advantage we give the enemy, he will claim more. Our only safety is to reject firmly the first insinuation to presumption. God has given us grace through the merits of Christ sufficient to withstand Satan, and be more than conquerors. Resistance is success. "Resist the devil, and he will flee from you." Resistance must be firm and steadfast. We lose all we gain if we resist today only to yield tomorrow.[10]

Summary

The apostle Peter passes on to his fellow elders the charge that Jesus had given to him, "Feed My sheep." Along with the charge, Peter invites the leaders of God's church to reexamine their motives for assuming spiritual leadership. He assures them that if faithful to their responsibilities, they will receive a crown of glory.

He then calls his readers to stiff resistance against the temptations of the devil, especially as they face the climactic

events of the great controversy. Finally, he closes his instruction with a benediction: "The God of all grace, who hath called us unto his eternal glory by Christ Jesus, after that ye have suffered a while, make you perfect, stablish, strengthen, settle you. To him be glory and dominion for ever and ever. Amen" (1 Peter 5:10, 11).

---

1. *Manuscript Releases*, vol. 12, p. 327.
2. William Barclay, *The Letters of James and Peter* (Philadelphia: Westminster Press, 1976), pp. 265, 266.
3. *Seventh-day Adventist Bible Commentary*, vol. 3, p. 1149.
4. *Testimonies for the Church*, vol. 2, pp. 286, 287.
5. *Notebook Leaflets From the Elmshaven Library*, vol. 1, p. 46.
6. *Manuscript Releases*, vol. 18, p. 139.
7. *The Desire of Ages*, p. 131.
8. *Testimonies for the Church*, vol. 2, p. 409.
9. Ibid., pp. 408, 409.
10. *Our High Calling*, p. 95.